Stem Cells

by Melissa Abramovitz

LUCENT BOOKS
A part of Gale, Cengage Learning

GALE
CENGAGE Learning·

Detroit • New York • San Francisco • New Haven, Conn • Waterville, Maine • London

LIBRARY OF CONGRESS CATALOGING-IN-PUBLICATION DATA

Abramovitz, Melissa, 1954-
  Stem cells / by Melissa Abramovitz.
    p. cm. -- (Hot topics)
  Summary: "The books in this series objectively and thoughtfully explore topics of political, social, cultural, economic, moral, historical, or environmental importance"-- Provided by publisher.
  Includes bibliographical references and index.
  ISBN 978-1-4205-0748-5 (hardback)
  1. Stem cells--Juvenile literature. 2. Embryonic stem cells--Juvenile literature. I. Title.
  QH588.S83.A27 2012
  616.02'774--dc23
                                                      2012004566

Lucent Books
27500 Drake Rd.
Farmington Hills, MI 48331

ISBN-13: 978-1-4205-0748-5
ISBN-10: 1-4205-0748-6

Printed in the United States of America
1 2 3 4 5 6 7 16 15 14 13 12

CONTENTS

FOREWORD   4

INTRODUCTION   6
Epic Discoveries and Controversies

CHAPTER 1   13
The Potential of Stem Cells

CHAPTER 2   30
The Controversy over Embryonic Stem Cells

CHAPTER 3   44
Alternatives to Embryonic Stem Cells

CHAPTER 4   62
Controversies over Cloning

CHAPTER 5   77
Who Should Regulate Scientific and Ethical Decisions?

CHAPTER 6   94
The Future of Stem Cell Research

NOTES   106

DISCUSSION QUESTIONS   113

ORGANIZATIONS TO CONTACT   115

FOR MORE INFORMATION   120

INDEX   122

PICTURE CREDITS   128

ABOUT THE AUTHOR   128

FOREWORD

Young people today are bombarded with information. Aside from traditional sources such as newspapers, television, and the radio, they are inundated with a nearly continuous stream of data from electronic media. They send and receive e-mails and instant messages, read and write online "blogs," participate in chat rooms and forums, and surf the Web for hours. This trend is likely to continue. As Patricia Senn Breivik, the former dean of university libraries at Wayne State University in Detroit, has stated, "Information overload will only increase in the future. By 2020, for example, the available body of information is expected to double every 73 days! How will these students find the information they need in this coming tidal wave of information?"

Ironically, this overabundance of information can actually impede efforts to understand complex issues. Whether the topic is abortion, the death penalty, gay rights, or obesity, the deluge of fact and opinion that floods the print and electronic media is overwhelming. The news media report the results of polls and studies that contradict one another. Cable news shows, talk radio programs, and newspaper editorials promote narrow viewpoints and omit facts that challenge their own political biases. The World Wide Web is an electronic minefield where legitimate scholars compete with the postings of ordinary citizens who may or may not be well-informed or capable of reasoned argument. At times, strongly worded testimonials and opinion pieces both in print and electronic media are presented as factual accounts.

Conflicting quotes and statistics can confuse even the most diligent researchers. A good example of this is the question of whether or not the death penalty deters crime. For instance, one study found that murders decreased by nearly one-third when the death penalty was reinstated in New York in 1995. Death penalty supporters cite this finding to support their argument that the existence of the death penalty deters criminals from committing murder. However, another study found that states without the death penalty have murder rates below the national average. This study is cited by opponents of capital punishment, who reject the claim that the death penalty deters murder. Students need context and clear, informed discussion if they are to think critically and make informed decisions.

The Hot Topics series is designed to help young people wade through the glut of fact, opinion, and rhetoric so that they can think critically about controversial issues. Only by reading and thinking critically will they be able to formulate a viewpoint that is not simply the parroted views of others. Each volume of the series focuses on one of today's most pressing social issues and provides a balanced overview of the topic. Carefully crafted narrative, fully documented primary and secondary source quotes, informative sidebars, and study questions all provide excellent starting points for research and discussion. Full-color photographs and charts enhance all volumes in the series. With its many useful features, the Hot Topics series is a valuable resource for young people struggling to understand the pressing issues of the modern era.

INTRODUCTION

Epic Discoveries and Controversies

Many devastating diseases result from cell destruction or degeneration, and humans have long sought cures for these types of ailments. Landmark discoveries in 1961, 1998, and 2007 opened and expanded a new field of medicine, called regenerative or cell-based medicine, that has the potential to treat and cure many such disorders. These discoveries also unleashed impassioned controversies that have drawn doctors, scientists, patients, theologians (experts who study religion), lawmakers, bioethicists (experts who study medical ethics issues), and the general public into a continuing battle over morality and research funding. The discoveries and controversies center on the stem cells from which other living cells develop.

The Search Begins

The work of the German doctor Rudolf Virchow, known as the "father of cellular medicine," in the late 1800s provided the basis for the search for precursor cells that give rise to other cells. Precursor cells are immature cells from which more specialized, mature cells develop. Virchow was the first to formally propose that every cell originates from another cell. Scientists in the early 1900s began searching for these precursor cells, but it was not until the mid-1900s that answers started to emerge.

After the 1945 atomic bombings of Nagasaki and Hiroshima, Japan, during World War II, doctors began studying ways to heal people exposed to radiation, and this research ultimately led to the discovery of stem cells. Physicians discovered that many people who initially survived the bombings died afterward because of radiation sickness. The radiation damaged blood-forming cells in the bone marrow. Bone marrow is the soft, spongy tissue inside bones. Cells in the bone marrow develop into the red, white, and platelet blood cells that must be continuously replenished for people to stay alive. The radiation also caused mutations in normal cells that led to cancer.

Rudolf Virchow's work provided the basis for the search for precursor cells. As a result, the German doctor became known as the father of cellular medicine.

Experiments on mice in 1951 showed that injecting animals that received radiation with healthy bone marrow prevented them from dying from radiation sickness. Subsequent studies showed that this also helped human radiation victims. Other experiments found that radiation could be used to kill off cancer cells before healthy bone marrow was transplanted to treat blood cancers.

While studying the use of radiation to prepare mice for bone marrow transplants, the Canadian researchers James Till and Ernest McCulloch at the Ontario Cancer Institute administered lethal radiation doses to mice, followed by bone marrow injections. The team discovered that the mice developed colonies of blood cells in their spleens, and that each colony was genetically identical to the bone marrow cells that had been injected. They realized this meant the bone marrow contained cells that could replicate and generate new, functioning blood cells, and they isolated the bone marrow cells and named them stem cells. Till and McCulloch published their findings in 1961, and in 1963 they went on to define two unique properties of stem cells: their ability to replicate (duplicate themselves) and their capacity to differentiate (develop into specific types of body cells).

Till and McCulloch became known as the "fathers of stem cell research." Christopher Paige, a physician at the Ontario Cancer Institute, states, "It's impossible to overstate the enormity of Till's and McCulloch's discovery. Their work changed the course of cancer research and lit the way to what we now call regenerative medicine—the use of stem cells for bone marrow transplants and many other types of disease research."[1]

Another Type of Stem Cell

Till and McCulloch's discovery instigated new stem cell research throughout the world, and in the late 1960s scientists discovered that animal embryos contained a different type of stem cell than the adult stem cells (ASCs) the Canadian researchers had identified. Unlike ASCs, these embryonic stem cells (ESCs) were pluripotent—that is, they could differentiate into any type of body cell.

In 1998 biologist James Thomson and his colleagues at the University of Wisconsin made another quantum leap in stem cell research when they extracted and cultured human ESCs taken from discarded embryos donated by in vitro fertilization (IVF) clinics. A culture consists of cells grown in a laboratory in a petri dish. Scientists place the cells in a culture medium, or chemicals that nourish the cells, to help them grow. IVF clinics are medical centers that specialize in helping women who are having trouble getting pregnant conceive babies. The term *in vitro* means "in a glass." Thus, doctors in an IVF clinic remove the woman's eggs from her body and fertilize them with her partner's sperm in a test tube. They then implant fertilized eggs into her womb.

Thomson's group grew five embryonic stem cell lines (a cell line consists of the cells that arise from a single dividing cell) derived from single embryos and found that the cells could continue to divide without differentiating for six months to two years under the right cell culture conditions. The researchers realized that if scientists could control the capacity of these cells to multiply and to later develop into certain cell types, ESCs had the potential to replace any body cells that had been damaged or destroyed by disease or injury.

But along with numerous potential therapeutic uses, Thomson's discovery triggered a firestorm of protest, particularly from religious conservatives, because it involved the destruction of human embryos. Many who oppose stem cell research believe that human embryos represent human lives and therefore should be protected from harm and destruction. Some argue that human embryos are entitled to the same human rights that people enjoy. They base this argument on the belief that human life begins at conception and that although an embryo undergoes numerous changes before it becomes a baby, the embryo is still the same individual that is recognized in later stages of life.

Thomson himself revealed in a newspaper article years later that he was aware that using embryos for research held ethical dilemmas, but that he had decided to proceed because of the immense potential to cure disease. "If human embryonic stem cell research does not make you at least a little bit uncomfortable, you have not thought about it enough," said Thomson. "I thought long and hard about whether I would do it."[2]

Scottish scientist Ian Wilmut poses with Dolly the sheep. Dolly was the first cloned mammal.

Cloning for Cells

Later research by other scientists led to another technique, called therapeutic cloning, for obtaining ESCs, and this innovation created new controversies over the morality and safety of cloning. Much of the debate over therapeutic cloning stems from the fact that the initial steps in creating the embryos from which ESCs are harvested are identical to those involved in reproductive cloning. Reproductive cloning is used to duplicate entire organisms.

Ever since the Scottish scientist Ian Wilmut succeeded in cloning the first mammal, a sheep named Dolly, in 1996, many people have been alarmed about the possibility of cloning humans. Reproductive cloning often leads to severe medical problems and birth defects in animals, and many people believe that cloning humans would be wrong for these and moral reasons as well.

Although therapeutic cloning only seeks to duplicate biological material for research purposes without creating new organisms, many who oppose any type of cloning consider it to be immoral. Scientists who advocate therapeutic cloning, on the other hand, claim that it should be allowed, since its goals are different than those of reproductive cloning.

The Newest Type of Stem Cell

Controversies over human ESCs and the methods used to obtain them led scientists to pursue alternative sources of pluripotent cells and new methods of using ASCs for treatments. In 2007 three independent teams of researchers announced that they had successfully reprogrammed ASCs to become pluripotent, and they named these cells induced pluripotent stem cells (iPSCs). The teams were led by Shinya Yamanaka of Japan, Rudolf Jaenisch of the Massachusetts Institute of Technology, and James Thomson of the University of Wisconsin. Opponents of embryonic stem cell research claim that the potential of iPSCs has made ESC research unnecessary.

Many scientists, including Thomson, and others embroiled in the embryonic stem cell debate believed iPSCs would not only make the need for ESCs go away, but would also overcome potential problems with patients' immune systems' rejecting ESCs. This is because the immune system attacks foreign tissue but generally tolerates cells it recognizes as "self." Theoretically iPSCs can be custom-made for each individual, since they come from the person's skin cells, whereas ESCs come from embryos.

However, scientific findings have led most experts today to conclude that ESCs, ASCs, and iPSCs are still important for basic research, such as testing new drugs, understanding how diseases develop, and understanding normal human development, as well as for potential treatments, and research with all of these continues. IPSCs themselves have raised new safety issues and ethical concerns, and debates about stem cell research and questions about who should have the power to make scientific and ethical decisions in the face of rapidly progressing technology remain robust.

THE POTENTIAL OF STEM CELLS

S tem cells have potential uses for treating and curing many devastating diseases, as well as for testing new drugs and for understanding how diseases develop. The magnitude of this potential is one issue that underlies the passionate stem cell–related controversies. In order to understand how stem cells can be used, it is important to understand how and why cells are essential for life.

Why Are Cells So Important?

All cells, which are the basic units of life, develop from stem cells, and normal cell function is essential for growth and continued operation. The nucleus, or center, of each cell contains deoxyribonucleic acid (DNA) molecules organized into genes that encode instructions for cell operations. Cellular DNA copies its genetic instructions onto ribonucleic acid (RNA) molecules, which translate and transmit these instructions to other parts of the cell that manufacture needed proteins and other chemicals. This process is known as gene expression. Different genes are expressed in different cells, which is why different types of cells have different functions. Inborn or acquired damage (mutations) to DNA or to the processes involved in gene expression can lead to many diseases.

Humans and animals are made of hundreds of kinds of cells. Some remain in the body throughout life, while others, such as blood cells, die regularly and are replaced by new cells that develop from stem cells. The author of *Stem Cell Now* explains that stem cells play a role in growth and cell replacement at all stages of life: "For an animal to grow and form larger structures, such as tissues and organs, stem cells need to produce large quantities of new cells. In the mature organism, stem cells replace and re-plenish cells that are injured as well as those that have grown old and died."[3]

Qualities of Stem Cells

The embryonic stem cells that underlie growth and development in embryos and the adult, or somatic, stem cells found in more mature tissue share several qualities but differ in other respects. ASCs are not just found in adults; they also exist in fetuses, babies, and children. The term *adult* in this instance means "nonembryonic," rather than fully grown.

According to the National Institutes of Health (NIH), "All stem cells—regardless of their source—have three general properties: they are capable of dividing and renewing themselves for long periods; they are unspecialized; and they can give rise to specialized cell types."[4] The differences occur in the degree of these attributes. ESCs grow much more readily and for longer

Adult stem cells and embryonic stem cells have some differences.

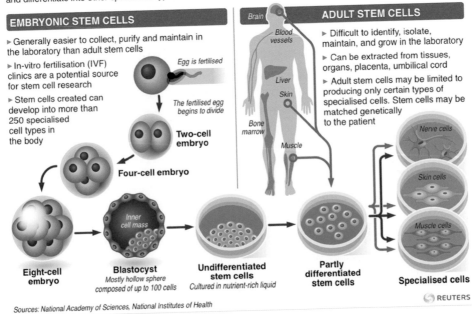

STEM CELLS FOR THERAPY

Stem cells are generally early stage cells that have the ability to continuously replicate themselves and differentiate into other specialised types of cells. There are two main categories of stem cells:

EMBRYONIC STEM CELLS

▸ Generally easier to collect, purify and maintain in the laboratory than adult stem cells

▸ In-vitro fertilisation (IVF) clinics are a potential source for stem cell research

▸ Stem cells created can develop into more than 250 specialised cell types in the body

Egg is fertilised

The fertilised egg begins to divide

Two-cell embryo

Four-cell embryo

Inner cell mass

Eight-cell embryo

Blastocyst
Mostly hollow sphere composed of up to 100 cells

Undifferentiated stem cells
Cultured in nutrient-rich liquid

Brain
Blood vessels
Liver
Skin
Bone marrow
Muscle

Partly differentiated stem cells

ADULT STEM CELLS

▸ Difficult to identify, isolate, maintain, and grow in the laboratory

▸ Can be extracted from tissues, organs, placenta, umbilical cord

▸ Adult stem cells may be limited to producing only certain types of specialised cells. Stem cells may be matched genetically to the patient

Nerve cells

Skin cells

Muscle cells

Specialised cells

REUTERS

Sources: National Academy of Sciences, National Institutes of Health

periods of time in cell cultures than ASCs do, although if they are grown for too long, mutations tend to accumulate in ESCs. ESCs are also pluripotent—they can give rise to any type of body cell. Most ASCs are multipotent—capable of developing into only a few different types of specialized cells.

The degree of potency, also known as plasticity, of stem cells changes gradually during embryonic development. Potency refers to the cell's flexibility to develop into different types of specialized cells. Contact among embryonic cells, along with genetically determined chemical signals, govern the stages of potency. During each phase, ESCs become increasingly committed to differentiating into certain cell types; that is, they become less potent or flexible. Scientists refer to newly fertilized eggs (zygotes) as totipotent—able to develop into all body cells. After about five days, zygotes become early embryos known as blastocysts, which consist of about two hundred cells. The blastocyst contains an inner cell mass of stem cells and an outer area called the trophoblast, which develops into the placenta that will encase the embryo. The inner cell mass stem cells are pluripotent, which is so similar to totipotency that the distinction is often confusing; totipotent cells can develop into an entire organism, while pluripotent cells can only develop into any of the cells that make up the organism.

About two weeks after fertilization, the inner mass cells organize themselves into three germ (embryonic cell) layers: the ectoderm, mesoderm, and endoderm. Ectoderm cells gradually develop into nerve and skin cells; mesoderm cells into blood, muscle, heart, and bone cells; and endoderm into most internal organs. After about eight weeks of embryonic development, the stem cells are fully committed to becoming only a few specialized cell types and can be classified as being multipotent.

Stem Cells and Treatment

Thus far, only multipotent stem cells have been used in nonexperimental medical treatments, in large part because injecting them usually leads to their migration to the area of the body from which they came. On the other hand, injecting or otherwise transplanting pluripotent cells without first inducing them to differentiate into a certain type of cell leads to the formation of tumors called teratomas, which are described in the book *The Stem Cell Divide* as being "the ugliest thing in medicine—a ghastly mixture of cells."[5] Teratomas contain a mishmash of cells and tissue—such as skin, bone, hair, and teeth—encased in a tumor, the result of pluripotent cells differentiating in an uncontrolled manner. Until scientists develop methods of reliably directing the differentiation of pluripotent stem cells, their therapeutic uses are considered experimental, rather than being approved treatments as those with ASCs are.

STEM CELLS WILL SHAPE THE FUTURE

"Stem cell research, and regenerative medicine generally, will have as much impact on our lives in the 21st century as did motor cars, antibiotics, and computers in the 20th."—Jonathan Slack, director of the University of Minnesota Stem Cell Institute

Quoted in University of Minnesota Stem Cell Institute. "Welcome to the Stem Cell Institute." www.stemcell.umn.edu.

Hematopoietic (blood-forming) stem cell transplants are a type of multipotent ASC transplant that doctors have been performing since the 1970s to treat blood cancers, other blood disorders, some immune disorders, and some other types of cancer. Physicians obtain hematopoietic stem cells from the patient's blood, a donor's blood or bone marrow, or donated umbilical cord blood, which is a rich source of stem cells. When stem cells are obtained from the patient's blood or a donor's blood, doctors first administer drugs that stimulate the bone marrow to produce and release stem cells into the bloodstream, since normally, insufficient numbers of stem cells are found in the blood. After sufficient quantities of stem cells are generated, doctors collect blood through a catheter and run it through an apheresis machine that separates out the stem cells and returns the blood to the person's body.

When bone marrow from a donor is used as a source of stem cells, doctors extract marrow from a hip bone using a large needle. Any donor's blood and tissue type must be compatible with the recipient to reduce the chances that the recipient's body will reject the transplant. Even then recipients must still take drugs to suppress the immune system to avoid rejection, and this can be dangerous because it impairs the individual's ability to fight infections. Transplanted donor cells can also attack the recipient's body in a potentially fatal complication known as graft-versus-host disease.

Once stem cells are harvested, they are frozen until after the patient receives radiation and chemotherapy to destroy the diseased bone marrow and cancer cells. Then doctors thaw and infuse the new cells into the patient, and ideally these stem cells engraft, or settle into the person's bone marrow and begin producing new blood cells. Because of the risks of rejection, graft-versus-host disease, failure to engraft, and infection during radiation and chemotherapy destroying the immune system, stem cell transplants are considered to be risky procedures, even though they do save many lives. Survival rates following these transplants vary according to the disease, the specific transplant hospital, and the source of the stem cells used, but in the case of leukemia, as an example, anywhere from 10 to 65 percent of patients are alive five years after a transplant. Since patients who receive stem cell transplants have failed to respond to other therapies, the treatment saves these individuals from certain death.

THE POTENTIAL OF STEM CELLS IS NOT IMMEDIATE

"Stem cells offer exciting promise for future therapies, but significant technical hurdles remain that will only be overcome through years of intensive research."—National Institutes of Health

National Institutes of Health. "Stem Cell Basics." http://stemcells.nih.gov/info/basics/basics6.asp.

Doctors are hoping that further research with ESCs and iPSCs will lead to transplant methods that circumvent some of the risks found with using ASCs. They believe that ESCs are more likely to engraft than ASCs are, since they proliferate much more readily in cell cultures than ASCs do, and this may make it easier to obtain the millions of stem cells needed to make such transplants successful. Since iPSCs can be derived from each patient's own cells, this could eliminate the problems of rejection and graft-versus-host disease.

Potential Uses in Treating Heart Disease

Using stem cells to treat diseases other than blood diseases is still experimental, but progress is being made. Scientists are testing stem cells for use in many diseases, including heart disease, diabetes, arthritis, Parkinson's disease, and many others.

Treatment of heart disease, which affects over 60 million Americans and kills nearly twenty-six hundred each day, is one area where stem cells hold great promise. Researchers are studying how embryonic and adult stem cells can be used to replace heart cells that are damaged or killed by heart attacks and other forms of heart disease. Scientists at the Cleveland Clinic, for example, are testing the effectiveness of stem cells taken from heart attack patients' bone marrow or muscles and injected into the bloodstream or directly into the heart. Previous studies have indicated that similar transplants sometimes improve heart function, but doctors do not yet know why this happens, nor are they sure about how to ideally prepare and administer the cells for best results.

According to the NIH publication *Regenerative Medicine*, there are conflicting theories about how and why stem cells may be effective for treating heart disease. The publication states:

> The mechanism by which stem cells promote cardiac repair remains controversial. . . . Initially, scientists believed that transplanted cells differentiated into cardiac cells, blood vessels, or other cells damaged by CVD [cardiovascular disease]. However, this model has been recently supplanted by the idea that transplanted stem cells release growth factors and other molecules that promote blood vessel formation or stimulate resident cardiac stem cells to repair damage.[6]

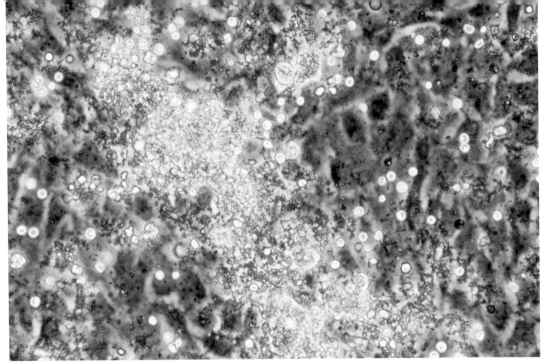

A light micrograph of cardiomyocytes, or heart muscle stem cells. These cells may be used in the future to manufacture new heart muscle tissue to replace damaged heart cells.

While doctors continue to debate how stem cells contribute to healing the heart, they also continue experiments to determine how best to use these cells.

Promising Research into Diabetes

Another widespread devastating disease for which stem cells hold promise is type 1 diabetes, which affects over 3 million Americans. Type 1 diabetes results from the immune system destroying cells in the pancreas called beta or islet cells, usually during childhood or adolescence. These cells produce insulin, a hormone needed so body cells can take up glucose from the blood. Without insulin, blood sugar levels rise to dangerous levels, poisons build up in the blood, and coma and death rapidly result. People with the disease must inject synthetic (human-made) insulin several times each day to stay alive.

Even with treatment, diabetes can lead to devastating complications such as blindness, kidney failure, heart disease, limb amputations, and nerve damage. Diabetes and its complications kill one American every three minutes.

The Basis of Stem Cell Hype

Bioethicist Arthur Caplan of the University of Pennsylvania explains in a 2011 article in *Science Progress* that much of the hype over the therapeutic potential of stem cells has resulted from proponents of embryonic stem cell research responding to opponents' arguments and from the lack of public funding for such research in the United States. Caplan writes:

> There was such a bitter battle over funding, so one side was screaming that you can't kill embryos to try and save people and in response, the defenders of stem cell research began to say, "look, if you would let us do this research we can save lives.". . . It was in the heat of that political battle to score points that they [proponents] overstated the case. . . . Many scientists and their supporters favoring public funding of embryonic stem cell research had gone too far in hyping the prospects of rapid cures following right on the heels of generous government funding.

Arthur Caplan. "The Stem Cell Hype Machine." *Science Progress*, April 18, 2011. http://scienceprogress.org/2011/04/the-stem-cell-hype-machine.

Experts believe that stem cells may someday cure diabetes. "Type 1 diabetes is an appropriate candidate disease for stem cell therapy, as the causative [underlying] damage is localized [confined] to a particular cell type,"[7] states the NIH. This means that theoretically, only one type of cell needs to be replaced to cure the disease. Researchers have been experimenting with non–stem cell beta cell transplants since the 1980s, but the limited supply of donor tissue, tissue rejection, and the fact that the transplanted cells tend to stop working over time have led to hopes that stem cells will prove to be more effective.

One of the preeminent researchers in this field is molecular biologist Douglas Melton of the Harvard Stem Cell Institute. The fact that two of Melton's children have diabetes has given him a personal incentive to pursue studies using ESCs, iPSCs, and other body cells as potential sources of insulin-producing cells. In 2009 Melton succeeded in reprogramming mature pancreatic cells that do not produce insulin into cells that do produce this hormone.

Other researchers are experimenting with coaxing stem cells found in the pancreas, liver, spleen, brain, and bone marrow into differentiating into beta cells. Thus far, no one has developed a method of reliably directing this differentiation; when beta cells are created and transplanted, they tend to die. Another significant hurdle that must be overcome is that since type 1 diabetes is caused by the patient's immune system destroying beta cells, methods of ensuring that the immune system will not destroy transplanted beta cells must be developed. But other than somehow replacing these cells, scientists have not come up with viable methods of curing diabetes.

Diseases of the Nervous System

Diseases and injuries affecting the nervous system are especially devastating because they impact peoples' ability to think, feel, and move. Because of this, and because other treatments for these problems have not been successful, much stem cell research is devoted to this area. Scientists are looking for ways of treating disabling conditions such as Alzheimer's disease, Parkinson's disease, Lou Gehrig's disease, multiple sclerosis, and spinal cord injuries.

THE IMMENSE POTENTIAL OF STEM CELLS

"It is safe to say that no single area of biomedicine holds such great promise for improving human health."—Christopher Thomas Scott, executive director of the Stem Cells in Society program at the Stanford University Center for Biomedical Ethics

Christopher Thomas Scott. *Stem Cell Now.* New York: Penguin, 2006, p. 12.

Researchers have discovered that a limited number of adult neural (nerve) stem cells are found in the brains of people and animals, and they are looking for ways to induce these cells to multiply and develop into functioning neurons, or nerve cells. According to the NIH, "These findings are exciting because they suggest that the brain may contain a built-in mechanism to repair itself. Unfortunately, these new neurons are only generated in a

A neural stem cell (pictured) has the potential to replace damaged or lost brain cells.

few sites in the brain and turn into only a few specialized types of nerve cells."[8]

Studies on mice and rats with Parkinson's disease, which results from the death of neurons in an area of the brain called the substantia nigra, indicate that it may be possible to stimulate these neural cells to develop into specialized cells. In Parkinson's the cells that die are those that normally produce the neurotransmitter dopamine, which affects movement, thinking, and emotion. People with the disease have disabling tremors, rigid limbs, and cognitive problems. Doctors treat Parkinson's with a drug called levodopa, which the brain converts to dopamine, but it is often ineffective and can have serious side effects.

In 2000 researchers at the University of California–Irvine injected a growth factor called transforming growth factor alpha into the brains of mice and rats with Parkinson's to stimulate stem cell differentiation into dopamine-producing neurons. The investigators found that these new cells migrated to damaged areas of the brain and began functioning. Further research is under way in hopes that someday such techniques may work in humans.

Other researchers are experimenting with growing adult neural stem cells in a laboratory and transplanting them into the brains of people with Parkinson's. Doctors have tried transplanting cells taken from patients' own bodies and from aborted fetuses, but results thus far have been mixed, and rarely have significant improvements been achieved. Many scientists believe that human ESCs and iPSCs hold greater therapeutic promise than ASCs do for this disease. In 2004 researchers at the Sloan-Kettering Institute in New York succeeded in coaxing human ESCs to develop into dopamine-producing cells in a laboratory, using a combination of growth factors. Whether such cells can be safely transplanted into people remains to be seen.

Stem Cells and Spinal Cord Injuries

Another devastating nervous system problem for which stem cells may prove to be effective is spinal cord injuries. The fact that well-known actor Michael J. Fox has Parkinson's disease and created the Michael J. Fox Foundation for Parkinson's Research is partly responsible for widespread public interest and support for research targeting this disease. In a similar manner, the Christopher and Dana Reeve Foundation started by the late *Superman* actor and his late wife brought stem cell research targeting spinal cord injuries front and center. Reeve, who became a quadriplegic following a horse-riding accident in 1995, passionately advocated for stem cell research funding in the face of widespread controversy about this issue, but he died from heart failure in 2004, before such research could help him personally.

Some experts, however, believe the popular media has overstated the therapeutic potential of stem cells to become functioning brain cells, in part due to celebrities such as Reeve and Fox promoting these therapies. For example, an article in *Human Events* points out that Fox's optimism that increasing funding for stem cell research will yield cures for diseases like Parkinson's and Alzheimer's is refuted by several scientists. According to the article, "Australian scientists blasted the notion that stem cells could treat or cure Alzheimer's disease, explaining that it's a 'whole brain disease.' Peter Rathjen, head of Molecular Bio-sciences at the University of Adelaide, told the *Australian* [newspaper], 'It's bloody nonsense that stem cells might be able to cure Alzheimer's. We don't even know what causes it.'"[9]

Other experts state that the primary value of studying brain cells may lie in areas other than transplant medicine. In a BBC website article, for instance, researcher Steven Pollard of the Wellcome Trust Centre for Stem Cell Research at Cambridge University states, "With brain cells, it would be very unrealistic to build up patients' hopes that these could be used as a repair mechanism in transplants, but what they will do is become a very useful tool to understand the basic biology of disease."[10] Pollard bases this statement on the fact that his research has shown that brain and spinal cord injuries have complex causes that may not be fixable simply by transplanting cells.

Medical experts agree that spinal cord injuries, in particular, often involve damage to multiple cell types and that this complicates potential therapies. In some cases neurons themselves are destroyed, and axons (extensions on neurons that transmit electrical and chemical signals to other nerve cells) therefore cannot communicate. Researchers are thus attempting to replace these neurons with stem cells or to stimulate damaged neurons to grow new axons. A 2004 study at Johns Hopkins University demonstrated that the growth factors retinoic acid and sonic hedgehog, along with a chemical called dibutyryl cAMP, stimulated axon growth in ESCs grown in cultures and transplanted into rats, but further research is needed to assess whether this can reverse paralysis.

In other instances, axons remain intact but cannot transmit messages because a type of neuron support cell called oligodendrocytes are damaged. Oligodendrocytes make up the myelin sheath, which lines and insulates all axons and allows signal transmission to occur. Some researchers are thus trying to devise methods of replenishing oligodendrocytes. In 2000 scientists at Washington University School of Medicine coaxed ESCs to develop into oligodendrocytes and injected the cells into paralyzed rats. Some of the animals regained limited use of their hind legs, so, like proposed methods of stimulating axon growth, this avenue

Potential Uses of Stem Cells in Gene Therapy

Gene therapy involves inserting normal genes into cells to replace defective, disease-causing genes. The genes must be carried into the cell nucleus with a carrier called a vector. The most commonly used vectors are inactivated viruses, since viruses have the capacity to enter and infect cells. However, the use of viral vectors has led to devastating consequences in some instances, and gene therapy is thus progressing slowly. In 1999 an eighteen-year-old boy named Jesse Gelsinger died from an adverse reaction to a viral vector used in gene therapy meant to cure his genetic liver disease. In 2003 several children being treated for severe combined immunodeficiency disease (SCID) developed leukemia after viral vectors activated cancer-causing genes in their cells.

Thus, scientists are seeking safer vectors, and many believe stem cells may hold the answer. In 2002 researchers at the Whitehead Institute for Biomedical Research in Massachusetts cured a genetic immune disorder in mice by inserting healthy genes into embryonic stem cells and transplanting the cells into the mice. Other doctors have cured several children with SCID by correcting the genetic defect in the children's hematopoietic stem cells in a laboratory and infusing the stem cells into their bloodstream. Further research using both embryonic and adult stem cells for this purpose is under way.

of investigation holds promise for treating spinal cord injuries and other neurological disorders.

However, while researchers continue to make progress, many scientists and bioethicists point out that both the media and some doctors continue to hype the notion that stem cell cures for neurological disorders are right around the corner or have already been achieved, only to disappoint patients because the science behind the treatment has not yet been perfected. For example, in 2004 doctors in South Korea injected umbilical cord blood stem cells into the spine of a paraplegic named Hwang Mi Soon. Hwang was soon able to stand and take a few steps with the aid of a walker. Newspapers throughout the world proclaimed that paralysis could now be cured. However, the results did not last; within a few weeks Hwang could no longer stand.

Doctors never figured out what went wrong but theorized that perhaps the injection itself had temporarily stimulated nerve activity. But when they looked at Hwang's spinal cord a month after the transplant, they saw signs of nerve regeneration that gave them hope. They decided to try again, on the assumption that injecting more stem cells might lead to permanent improvement. Again, the results were minimal and short-lived, and Hwang also developed pain and an infection in her spine.

Other Uses for Stem Cells

While the full therapeutic potential of stem cells may not be realized immediately or ever, these cells can (and in some cases already do) help scientists in other ways. One potential use is in making gene therapy, which involves replacing defective genes with normal ones, safer and more effective. Another application is in testing the effectiveness of new drugs. In the past, researchers could only test drugs on laboratory animals before beginning clinical trials with humans. Sometimes, though, a drug that seems safe in animals is harmful to people. Testing the drug on human cells derived from ESCs, ASCs, or iPSCs can give a better indication of how people will respond.

Another valuable use of stem cells comes from studying how stem cells differentiate and from analyzing stem cells grown from people with certain diseases. Cancers, birth defects, and many other disorders result from abnormal cell development, and understanding how these abnormalities come about can help devise methods of prevention and treatment. Experts refer to this use of stem cells as modeling disease in a test tube. In April 2011 researchers at the Salk Institute in La Jolla, California, reported progress in this regard when they published a study in which they transformed skin cells taken from schizophrenic patients into iPSCs, turned the iPSCs into nerve cells, and tracked the cellular development of abnormalities that led to schizophrenia. Lead researcher Fred Gage said in a newspaper article, "This is the first time that a complex mental disease has been modeled in live human cells."[11]

Other scientists are gaining insight into normal human development by studying human stem cells. A team of scientists at the

University of Wisconsin, for example, is studying how hormones affect ESC differentiation, and researchers at the University of California–San Francisco are investigating how certain genes stimulate ESC differentiation into germ (reproductive) cells. Such research has potential applications for developing stem cell treatments as well as for preventing some diseases from occurring.

Stephen Howarth, who suffers from a genetic eye condition, has had his full vision restored after gene therapy treatment. The gene therapy replaced Howarth's faulty gene with an artificially created one.

Controversies over Potential

With the unprecedented potential uses of stem cells, passions run strong among people who see stem cells as providing their best hope of effective disease treatment. But equally passionate individuals argue that some types of stem cell research are morally wrong, and such controversies, along with significant scientific and safety hurdles (such as directing stem cell differentiation, tissue rejection, and controlling cell growth), must be overcome before the potential of stem cells can be realized.

THE POTENTIAL OF STEM CELLS HAS BEEN HYPED

"There has been hype and overpromising. . . . I don't know if stem cell research will work, I think it's very interesting, I support doing it, but I think you have to be honest and say there's a small chance nothing will work."—Bioethicist Arthur Caplan, director of the Center for Bioethics at the University of Pennsylvania

Arthur Caplan. "The Stem Cell Hype Machine." *Science Progress*, April 18, 2011. www.scienceprogress.org/2011/04/the-stem-cell-hype-machine.

Few people dispute the fact that stem cells, and the discipline called regenerative or cell-based medicine that they have launched, offer some of the most promising avenues of treatment in medical science today. The NIH explains:

> Perhaps the most important potential application of human stem cells is the generation of cells and tissues that could be used for cell-based therapies. Today, donated organs and tissues are often used to replace ailing or destroyed tissue, but the need for transplantable tissues and organs far outweighs the available supply. Stem cells, directed to differentiate into specific cell types, offer the possibility of a renewable source of replacement cells and tissues.[12]

But some people believe this potential has been exaggerated and portrayed as capable of producing immediate results in order to garner support for controversial procedures. One expert who holds this view is biologist Joseph Panno, who states in his book *Stem Cell Research*, "In their enthusiasm for these therapies, many scientists have given the general public an unrealistic impression of what can actually be achieved. In theory, of course, the sky is always the limit, but scientists interested in using stem cells to repair damaged organs fail to make it clear that there are serious obstacles to overcome before these therapies become a reality."[13]

Despite the debates over whether the potential of stem cells has been hyped, most individuals on both sides of the issue support continuing some form of stem cell research because the consensus is that, even with obstacles that must be overcome, the chances that someday stem cells will ease widespread suffering is too promising to overlook. However, impassioned controversies over which types of stem cell research should be allowed continue to influence the direction and progress of this research.

THE CONTROVERSY OVER EMBRYONIC STEM CELLS

Much of the controversy surrounding stem cells centers on human embryonic stem cells because the process of obtaining these cells kills an embryo. Scientists obtain ESCs by extracting them from embryos discarded or donated from in vitro fertilization (IVF) clinics. In IVF, doctors take eggs, or oocytes, from a woman and fertilize them with a man's sperm in a test tube. They then transfer fertilized eggs into the woman's uterus in hopes that one will implant in the uterine wall and develop into a baby. But many times, the embryo does not implant and pregnancy does not occur. This is why fertility doctors fertilize several eggs in a laboratory and freeze them for future use if they are needed.

Once a successful pregnancy occurs, the parents may elect to leave any unused fertilized eggs in frozen storage, to dispose of them as medical waste, or to donate them for scientific research. When they are donated for research, scientists thaw the cells and, after five to seven days, when the blastocyst is about the size of a grain of sand and contains about two hundred pluripotent cells, they extract stem cells from the inner cell mass. They then transfer the cells to a laboratory culture dish containing a nutrient broth and a layer of mouse cells called feeder cells. Feeder cells contain substances that help stem cells grow but also keep the stem cells in an undifferentiated state. Researchers also add chemicals called transcription factors to further prevent the cells from differentiating. The stem cells begin to divide and proliferate into a cell line. When the cells cover the petri dish, technicians remove some cells and place them in new dishes to form subcultures. Over many months the original cells can yield millions of new cells that can be subcultured or frozen and sent to other research laboratories.

Researchers never obtain ESCs from a woman's body, so ESCs used in research do not destroy an embryo growing in a woman's womb. But because extracting stem cells from a blastocyst prevents the embryo from potentially growing into a baby, many people view this as terminating a life. Those opposed to using ESCs believe that, like abortion, destroying an embryo for any purpose is murder, since it willfully ends the existence of a human life in its earliest form.

Pro-life protesters participate in a demonstration against the use of embryonic stem cells in medical research.

When Does Life Begin?

The primary focus of the controversies surrounding the use of human ESCs revolves around the question of when life begins and whether an embryo is a human life. Scientists and philosophers throughout history have debated this question. The ancient Greek philosopher Aristotle put forth the view that embryos are in a vegetative state after conception and an animate state when body parts begin to function, and that the intellectual state that makes someone human does not begin until after birth.

Many people today, including most scientists, at least partially agree with this assessment, and indeed the legal definition of a human being in the United States specifies that embryos and fetuses (which are embryos that are more than eight weeks old) are not people. However, laws still require that embryos and fetuses be treated ethically, and abortions, except in cases where the mother's life is in danger, are only permitted up to the fifth month of pregnancy.

IT IS IMMORAL TO USE DISCARDED EMBRYOS IN RESEARCH

"Human embryos are indeed human beings, and, as such, deserve a level of respect that is incompatible with treating them as disposable research material."—Robert P. George, professor of jurisprudence at Princeton University, and Patrick Lee, professor of bioethics at the Franciscan University of Steubenville

Robert P. George and Patrick Lee. "Embryonic Human Persons." *EMBO Reports*, April 2009. www.nature.com/embor/journal/v10/n4/full/embor200942.html.

Some individuals, primarily those who label themselves as "pro-life," however, believe that human life begins at the moment of conception, and that embryos and fetuses should be accorded the same rights and consideration as other people. Pro-lifers distinguish themselves from those who are pro-choice (in favor of each woman deciding for herself whether or not to continue a pregnancy or have an abortion). Those who support the pro-life viewpoint believe that no one should be allowed to terminate a human life and that it is incumbent upon lawmakers and others to prevent people from doing so, even when the life is not yet born. This viewpoint stems from the decree of Pope Pius IX in 1869 that life begins at conception. Prior to that time, the Catholic Church espoused the view of Saint Augustine that a fetus does not become a person until forty days after conception, when the soul enters the developing body.

Today the Catholic Church and some other religious groups officially support Pope Pius's doctrine, but some individuals within these groups disagree. For example, several polls have found that as many as 70 percent of Catholics support ESC research and do not believe an early embryo is a person. Other religious groups, such as the Presbyterians, Methodists, Episcopalians, Unitarians, and most Jewish sects, officially espouse the view that embryos are not human beings. Some believe an embryo becomes a person sometime during fetal development, while others state that a person does not come into existence until a baby is born and starts breathing. Many base the latter viewpoint on a passage in Genesis that reads, "Then the Lord God formed man from the dust of the ground, and breathed into his nostrils the breath of life; and the man became a living creature."[14]

Is an Embryo a Human Person?

People on both sides of the issue argue passionately over whether or not an embryo constitutes a person. Those who oppose the viewpoint that an embryo is a person from the moment of conception cite several arguments to support their beliefs. First of all, many doctors argue that fertilization, conception, and personhood are entirely different phenomena. Physician George Daley writes, "Biology itself does not support the notion of a 'moment' of conception. In fact, conception is a complex process that proceeds over many hours, and although a new genome is formed when the egg and sperm pro-nuclei fuse to become the single-celled human zygote, a unique biological individual is not apparent until later in human development."[15]

Physician Alan Malnak further discusses the medical definition of conception in a newspaper article, in which he writes, "Fertilization and conception are not synonymous and do not occur at the same time. Fertilization of an egg may occur naturally in the fallopian tube (in vivo) or in a piece of glass equipment by scientific means (in vitro). Conception occurs when a fertilized egg implants itself in a suitable uterine lining and begins to draw nourishment. A pregnancy does not actually begin until the process of conception is complete."[16]

Another argument advanced by pro–embryonic stem cell research advocates is that since an embryo can split into two and create twin embryos until two weeks after fertilization, the five- to seven-day-old blastocysts used as a source of stem cells cannot be considered to be a single human being.

In contrast, the opposing viewpoint holds that embryos are people from the moment of conception. In an article in the journal *EMBO Reports*, Robert P. George, a professor of jurisprudence at Princeton University, and Patrick Lee, a professor of bioethics at the Franciscan University of Steubenville in Ohio, write, "The human embryo is the same individual as the human organism at subsequent stages of development. . . . Organisms are not processes; rather they are entities that persist through time. When an organism comes into existence, it comes into existence as a whole organism—although at an immature stage. Just as you and I were once infants, so too you and I were once embryos."[17]

Furthermore, writes Josh Brahm of Right to Life of Central California, whether or not fertilization and conception are identical does not refute the fact that once they have occurred, a human being is formed. "HESCR [human embryonic stem cell research] kills human embryos after they're several days to a few weeks old. No matter how long the entire process of fertilization takes, it still results in a unique human being whose body parts are being exploited,"[18] Brahm writes.

A Group of Cells or Something More?

Other arguments that embryos are not people revolve around the notion that a blastocyst is an uncoordinated, undifferentiated group of cells, whereas a person is more than just a group of cells with human DNA; a person's cells are organized into specialized organs that function in a coordinated manner. "People are not genes. They are so much more than that,"[19] states embryologist Ian Wilmut, famed for cloning Dolly the sheep.

Other experts agree with the contention that the cells that make up a person are not actually the person. If cells were people, argue the British bioethicists Thomas Douglas and Julian Savulescu of the Uehiro Centre for Practical Ethics at Oxford University, then humans would mourn every time they lost hair or skin cells or

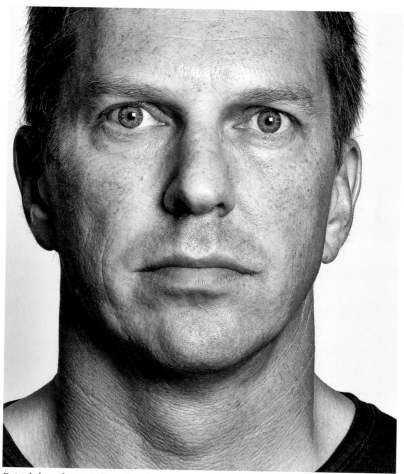

British bioethicist Julian Savulescu argues that embryonic stem cell research should not be considered unethical due to the fact that groups of immature cells should not be considered human.

had an organ removed. The fact that people faced with the choice of saving a child or thousands of frozen embryos in a fire would choose to save the child also illustrates the concept that the moral value of a fully functioning life is greater than that of a group of immature cells, write Douglas and Savulescu.

Using Discarded Embryos for Medical Research Is Moral

"The use of 'spare' or 'surplus' embryos from IVF clinics is ethically appropriate because they were created for procreative purposes that will no longer be fulfilled."—Bioethicist George J. Annas of the Health Law Department of the Boston University School of Public Health, bioethicist Arthur Caplan of the Center for Bioethics at the University of Pennsylvania, and physician Sherman Elias of the Department of Obstetrics and Gynecology at the University of Illinois

George J. Annas, Arthur Caplan, and Sherman Elias. "Stem Cell Politics, Ethics, and Medical Progress." *Nature Medicine*, December 1999, p. 1340.

Rutgers University philosophy professor Jeff McMahan writes that exactly when a group of cells becomes a person cannot be determined scientifically, but that differentiated cells working together in a coordinated manner are one prerequisite. "Whether we are organisms is not a scientific question," McMahan writes. "There is no experiment that can be done to determine whether or not we are organisms. . . . Since significant cell differentiation is clearly identifiable at around two weeks after conception, it seems reasonable to treat that as the time at which a human organism begins to exist."[20]

George and Lee, however, believe coordination is present even in blastocysts and that this means they "constitute a human organism, for they form a stable body and act together in a coordinated manner, which contributes to regular, predictable and determinate development toward the mature stage of a human being."[21] Scott Klusendorf of the pro-life group Stand to Reason further asserts that the value of a person cannot be determined by how mature or coordinated its body processes are. "If the entity itself is intrinsically valuable, then it must be so from the moment it exists. Nothing can be added to make it valuable,"[22] he writes. Because a human life is valuable by its nature, he goes on to state, destroying it at any stage is morally wrong.

"The Capacity for Consciousness"

McMahan and many other bioethicists and scientists also argue that even after cell differentiation begins, another critical point to consider in evaluating whether an embryo is a person is consciousness. McMahan writes, "Only after the development of the capacity for consciousness is there anyone who can be harmed, or wronged, by being killed."[23] Medical experts state that the earliest in embryonic development that consciousness is possible is between twenty-two and twenty-four weeks after conception, when neural connections in the brain develop.

However, George and Lee disagree that consciousness is a prerequisite for humanness. "It is clear that one need not be actually or immediately conscious, reasoning, deliberating or making choices, in order to be a human being who deserves full moral respect, for plainly people who are asleep or in reversible comas deserve such respect,"[24] they write.

Potential Human Beings

The phrase "potential human beings" is also often used in arguments for and against the morality of embryonic stem cell research. Many people argue that embryos are not human beings but do have the potential to develop into humans. Some who hold this view believe that since potential is not the same as actual, destroying an embryo does not constitute taking a life. Neuroscientist Michael Gazzaniga, for example, states, "It is meaningless to call a fertilized egg a potential human being. There's potential for 30 homes in a Home Depot, but if the Home Depot burns down, the headline isn't '30 Homes Burn Down.' It's 'Home Depot Burns Down.'"[25] McMahan expands this argument to conclude that killing an embryo is not the same as killing a person: "To kill an early embryo is not to kill someone like you or me. It is to prevent one of us from coming into existence."[26]

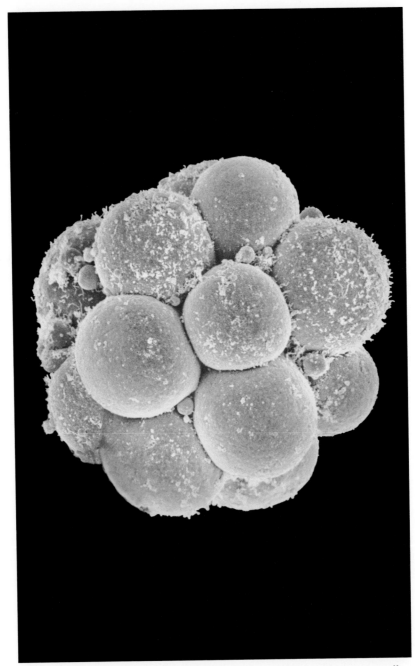

A colored scanning electron micrograph of a human embryo at the sixteen-cell stage. Some people argue that embryonic stem cell research is immoral because it destroys the developing embryo, and as a result, a potential human being.

Others who view embryos as potential human beings, on the other hand, argue that destroying this potential is morally wrong. Philosophy professor Bertha Manninen argues that since not granting an embryo the same rights as a fully developed person can result in substantial harm, it is wrong not to protect the embryo. "Since all innocent persons have a moral right to life, all potential innocent persons also have a moral right to life,"[27] she writes.

Still others, who believe a human being exists from the time of conception, reject the notion that an embryo is a potential person. "A human embryo is not a 'potential human being.' It *is* a human

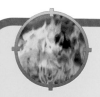

Bioethicists' Argument That Embryos Are Not People

Bioethicists Thomas Douglas and Julian Savulescu argue that embryos are not people, for several reasons. One reason, they say, relates to the human response to the fact that more than 220 million embryos per year die inside a woman's womb within eight weeks of conception. Douglas and Savulescu explain:

If we supposed that embryos were persons, we would have to conclude that more than 220 million people die each year due to spontaneous abortion [miscarriage]— which is more than seven times as many people as die from cancer. It would surely follow that we ought to do something to reduce this staggering death toll; we should

try to discover its biological basis and we should prioritize the development of therapeutics to prevent it given that it would be a greater cause of human death than all other causes combined. After all, we pour resources into the prevention of diseases—such as acquired immune deficiency disorder (AIDS) and cancer—that kill far fewer persons. It seems implausible that such reprioritization is morally required [because] our intuitions are incompatible with the view that embryos are persons.

Thomas Douglas and Julian Savulescu. "Destroying Unwanted Embryos in Research." *EMBO Reports*, 2009. www.nature.com/embor/journal/v10/n4/full/embor200954.html.

being,"[28] writes the group Canadian Physicians for Life. Such individuals thus argue that killing an embryo is taking a human life.

BLASTOCYSTS ARE NOT PEOPLE

"A living human organism is an entity with human genes that is composed of various living parts that function together in an integrated way to sustain a single life, and that is not itself a part of another living biological entity. The cells that compose an embryo do not yet serve sufficiently different functions to allow us to say that they are coordinated in the service of a single life."—Rutgers University philosophy professor Jeff McMahan

Jeff McMahan. "Killing Embryos for Stem Cell Research." *Metaphilosophy*, April 2007, p. 179.

Another argument for the view that destroying a blastocyst is far different from killing a person is put forth by Malnak, who explains that stem cells are taken from IVF blastocysts well before the time when the blastocyst would implant in a mother's uterus. Implantation occurs from one to two weeks after fertilization. Furthermore, about 60 percent of IVF blastocysts are not viable and would never implant or eventually develop into a baby. Thus, Malnak believes that using preimplantation blastocysts as a source of stem cells is in no way taking a life. Opponents, on the other hand, argue that the blastocyst is a potential person regardless of where it is.

Is Embryonic Stem Cell Research Moral?

Proponents of ESC research believe that their view that the embryos from which stem cells are extracted are not people, plus the potential to save many lives with stem cell therapy, justifies their support of such research. Even many who call themselves pro-life conservatives believe that the fact that a blastocyst does not have even a rudimentary nervous system is reason enough to support the notion that using ESCs for research is not morally wrong. Furthermore, the prevailing view among ESC research supporters is

Pro-life Versus Pro-choice

The debate between those who call themselves pro-life versus those who call themselves pro-choice originated with the 1973 Supreme Court *Roe v. Wade* decision, which legalized abortion. As technology advanced to the point of using machines to prolong life in brain-dead or comatose people, this issue became entangled in the debate between pro-life and pro-choice advocates. The pro-life view holds that people are morally obligated to preserve and respect all human life, regardless of the stage of development or quality of life, and that abortion or withdrawing life support from those in a vegetative state is murder. Pro-choice advocates believe individuals have the right to choose whether or not to prolong their own or a loved one's life if he or she has no chance of improving, and that women should have the right to choose whether or not to continue a pregnancy.

The main point of conflict between these two groups was the abortion issue, but since human embryonic stem cell research began, it has become an intricate part of the debate. However, not all pro-lifers who oppose abortion are opposed to ESC research. Some believe an early embryo is not a human being, but that a fetus in later stages of development is a person. The distinctions between pro-life and pro-choice have thus become blurred in the ESC debate.

Pro-life demonstrators confront pro-choice demonstrators during a 2006 rally. Both sides have strong opinions on stem cell research.

that a true pro-life position places more value on the potential to alleviate the suffering of millions of patients than on immature cells in a test tube. Senator Orrin Hatch of Utah is one politically conservative, pro-life individual who states, "I think that support of this research is a pro-life, pro-family position. This research holds out hope for more than 100 million Americans."[29]

BLASTOCYSTS ARE PEOPLE

"The embryo has the full complement of human genes and is worthy of the same dignity given to all members of the human family."—Statement of the U.S. Conference of Catholic Bishops

Quoted in Nancy Frazier O'Brien. "Embryonic Stem-Cell Research Immoral, Unnecessary, Bishops Say." American Catholic. www.americancatholic.org/News/StemCell/default.asp.

Many bioethicists and religious leaders also stress that ethics and religion compel people to combat human suffering. "Careful use of the human blastocyst may be seen as a basic human duty in the face of significant suffering. These are the reasons why people of the deepest faith all over the globe support and defend stem cell research,"[30] writes bioethicist Laurie Zoloth.

Another point many bioethicists and religious leaders make is that using stem cells taken from frozen embryos is far more productive than is discarding the embryos. Bioethicists George J. Annas, Arthur Caplan, and Sherman Elias write, "The choice of donating spare embryos for use in important medical research that cannot be done by other means is ethically superior to either destroying them or keeping them perpetually cryopreserved [frozen]."[31]

The Catholic Church, though, disagrees with this contention, stating, "The church opposes the direct destruction of innocent human life for any purpose, including research. These embryos will not die because they are inherently unable to survive, but because others are choosing to hand them over for destructive research."[32] The church also points out that since there are viable alternatives to using ESCs, there is no reason to kill embryos when ASCs and iPSCs are available.

Klusendorf offers another reason why he believes ESC research is morally wrong: It is a form of discrimination against those who are powerless to defend themselves. "In the past, we used to discriminate on the basis of skin color or gender, but now, with ESCR, we discriminate on the basis of size, level of development, location, and degree of dependency,"[33] he writes.

As the debate over ESC research continues, one positive result has been that research on other types of stem cells has advanced and may indeed yield answers to some of the therapeutic and moral hurdles.

ALTERNATIVES TO EMBRYONIC STEM CELLS

Controversies over the ethics of using human ESCs and the need to overcome the medical risks, such as teratomas and tissue rejection, posed by these cells have led scientists to seek other methods of obtaining stem cells for research and therapeutic purposes. Opponents of ESC research have pointed out that there are viable alternatives to ESCs, and this has spurred many researchers to experiment with other types of stem cells. It has also led some to pursue procuring ESCs without destroying embryos. But although most aspects of ASCs and iPSCs do not stir the ethical debates that have been a part of ESC research, several procedures associated with these types of stem cells have generated controversies of their own, and other moral concerns about methods of procuring ESCs without destroying embryos have emerged as well.

Stem Cell Lines from Single Cells

Robert Lanza and his colleagues at Advanced Cell Technology in Worcester, Massachusetts, are one group of researchers who have attempted to obtain ESCs without killing embryos. Usually, researchers extract the entire inner cell mass from a blastocyst to obtain ESCs. But in 2006 Lanza succeeded in establishing several human ESC lines from single cells taken from IVF blastocysts. However, very few of the cells lived to form a cell line. Then in 2008 his team achieved better results by taking a single cell from eight-cell embryos. At this stage, stem cells have not yet developed in the embryo. By adding a protein called laminin to the culture medium, the scientists were able to direct the single cells to develop into stem cells, and 20 to 50 percent developed into usable stem cell lines.

Since these techniques involve extracting only one cell, the embryos usually survive and can theoretically be transferred to a woman's womb to develop further. However, biologist Joseph Panno writes that Lanza's innovation is not likely to have advantages over other methods of obtaining embryonic cells: "Given the expense and the inefficiency of IVF, parents will likely choose embryos that have not been tampered with. Consequently, it appears that this new method of harvesting blastomeres has no practical application."[34]

Ethical concerns have also arisen over whether the single cells that were removed might have developed into people and about whether the technique harms the remaining embryonic cells. For

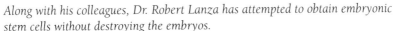

Along with his colleagues, Dr. Robert Lanza has attempted to obtain embryonic stem cells without destroying the embryos.

example, the Ethics & Religious Liberty Commission, a part of the Southern Baptist Convention that is dedicated to ensuring that Judeo-Christian values are upheld in public policy, has raised several moral objections to Lanza's procedure. The commission writes:

> While we appreciate Dr. Lanza's effort to find a way around the unacceptable destruction of human embryos to obtain embryonic stem cells, we do not consider his solution to be viable. We raise the following objections to his efforts: 1. The embryo could be destroyed in the process, and currently embryos are being destroyed in the process. 2. If one implants an embryo that has had a cell removed at its 8-cell stage, the embryo is absent about 12% of its original genetic material as it divides to form a mature human being. No one knows yet the consequences of this loss. 3. It is believed that sometimes a single cell does separate at this early stage naturally and creates a twin. 4. When one dismantles these cells or interrupts their development, they are killing a newly-formed embryo.[35]

In response to concerns that the procedure can harm an embryo, Lanza points out that the procedure is similar to the single-cell biopsy that fertility clinics often perform, known as preimplantation genetic diagnosis (PGD), to screen for genetic diseases in embryos. He notes that PGD is considered very safe, and that in his research the embryos used in the study "were frozen and remain alive,"[36] and that over 80 percent seemed normal afterward.

Story Landis, head of the NIH Stem Cell Task Force, challenges this assessment, stating that PGD reduces the number of pregnancies and live births from IVF embryos. "So yes, the embryos look fine, and yes, you do get pregnancies, but you don't get as many. From a legalistic view you would have to ask: How much harm is harm?"[37]

Stem Cells from Dead Embryos

Another technique that researchers devised to circumvent ethical concerns about destroying embryos involves extracting viable stem cells from dead embryos. During the IVF process, several of the embryos may fail to grow. Because these embryos are incapable of producing a viable pregnancy, they are routinely discarded as medical waste unless otherwise donated for research. In 2006 researchers at the University of Newcastle in England pioneered a method of procuring stem cells from discarded IVF embryos. The stem cells grew in cultures and were pluripotent, which means that they behaved like typical ESCs, even though they were extracted from dead embryos. As with single-cell extractions, however, this has raised new concerns and safety issues.

Individuals who believe that embryos are human beings tend to view the practice of taking cells from a dead embryo as similar to the unethical act of harvesting organs from a dead person who did not consent to the procedure. Another concern is over whether or not these discarded embryos are truly dead, because criteria for determining embryonic death are not universally agreed upon. Since embryos do not have brains or hearts, a lack of brain or heart function cannot be proof of death. Scientists state that an early embryo is considered dead if it stops dividing, but the Catholic Church, among others, believes that if live stem cells can be extracted, an embryo is not really dead.

Related safety concerns raised by stem cell experts include the probability that embryos that die naturally may be genetically abnormal, and any stem cells taken from this source might also be abnormal. The fact that the technique is inefficient at procuring live stem cells also makes it unlikely that this will ever be a preferred method of obtaining ESCs.

Parthenogenesis: Faking Fertilization

Another experimental method of obtaining embryonic stem cells is parthenogenesis, which involves stimulating an oocyte to function as though it were fertilized so it will begin to divide and form a blastocyst. Scientists use chemicals, rather than sperm, to activate an unfertilized oocyte taken from a donor. The resulting blastocyst can live for at least a few days, but no longer, because it is not a true embryo.

In 2007 Elena Revazova and Jeffrey Janus led a team at International Stem Cells in Oceanside, California, that used parthenogenesis to obtain embryonic stem cells. They named the cells human parthenogenetic stem cells (hpSCs). Since hpSCs are derived from a particular donor, they can potentially be immune-matched to avoid rejection if used therapeutically. The researchers also believe hpSCs can be coaxed into forming a variety of cell types, and they are currently experimenting with methods of achieving this goal.

Although obtaining hpSCs does not destroy a fertilized egg, many disapprove of the practice. For example, a March 2011 article in the Catholic publication *Zenit* explains that the Catholic Church opposes parthenogenesis for several reasons. First of all, the church considers any procedure, including IVF and any practices related to IVF, that tinkers with the natural process of reproduction to be an abuse of science. The article states: "The term "parthenogenesis" (from the Greek words "parthenos," virgin, and "genesis," birth) refers to a form of asexual reproduction, naturally occurring among some insects, birds, and lizards. . . . Since

In 2007 Dr. Jeffrey Janus (pictured) and his colleague Dr. Elena Revazova led a team of scientists that used parthenogenesis, an experimental method, to obtain embryonic stem cells. They named these cells human parthenogenetic stem cells (hpSCs).

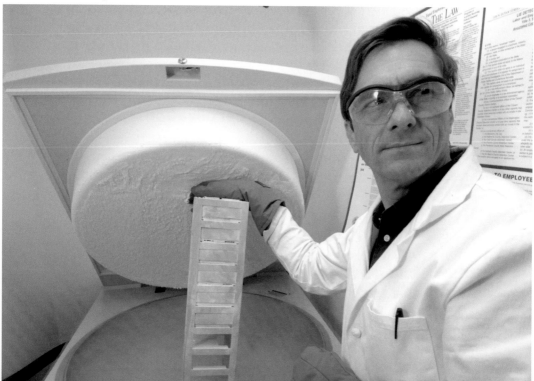

Magnetic Beads for Finding Adult Stem Cells

Isolating adult stem cells from other cells is difficult, but an invention by Norwegian scientist John Ugelstad called Dynabeads is helping with this process. Dynabeads are tiny magnetic beads used to separate cells, DNA, and proteins. If a scientist wishes to isolate hematopoietic stem cells, for example, he or she targets a surface protein called CD34, which all hematopoietic stem cells possess. The author of *The Stem Cell Divide* explains how the procedure, which utilizes a separator machine called an Isolex, works:

A quantity of the beads is slathered with an antibody that will stick to the CD34 cells, then introduced into the cellular mixture the way one would toss grains of barley into a cooking pot of soup. Once the CD34 cells have stuck to the magnetic beads, the Isolex is powered on to retrieve the beads, now coated with the CD34 cells which have glommed on to their surfaces.

Michael Bellomo. *The Stem Cell Divide*. New York: AMACOM, 2006, p. 165.

mammalian reproduction is sexual, parthenogenesis is a profoundly abnormal process." Another reason relates to the question of whether parthenogenesis creates an embryo, as the article explains: "Is it possible that in the process of activation the oocyte can transform into an embryo? The question is presently unsettled. . . . Unless we have moral certainty that a dividing parthenogenetically activated human oocyte is not an embryo, we have an obligation to avoid research with human parthenotes."[38]

Embryonic Germ Cells

Scientists have also found that embryonic germ (EG) cells, which normally develop into egg and sperm cells, are another source of stem cells. Researchers obtain EG cells from an area called the gonadal ridge on the back of eight- to twelve-week-old aborted fetuses. Once placed in a cell culture, EG cells become pluripotent, so they actually turn into stem cells that are similar to ESCs. The first scientist to extract and grow human EG cells was geneticist John Gearhart of Johns Hopkins University in 1998.

Gearhart went on to show that although cultured EG cells look like ESCs, they are slightly less pluripotent and do not form teratomas when injected into living creatures. They do, however, differentiate into cells from all three embryonic germ layers.

The fact that EG cells do not form teratomas may mean they are safer than ESCs for therapeutic use. Gearhart and his associates showed that injecting cultured mouse EG cells into paralyzed mice partially restored the ability to walk, but much more research is needed before these cells can be tested in humans. The fact that EG cells are derived from aborted fetuses has also raised ethical objections from groups opposed to abortion. While proponents of EG research point out that abortion is legal and that cells from an aborted fetus would go to waste if not used in research, opponents argue that abortion and any further desecration of a fetus that follows an abortion are immoral.

Sources of Nonembryonic Stem Cells

The ongoing controversy over ESCs has not only led scientists to explore new methods of obtaining ESCs, but has also fostered increased innovation and research on the other types of stem cells—ASCs and iPSCs. ASCs are noncontroversial, but ethical debates have arisen about one practice related to ASCs obtained from umbilical cord blood. The traditional practice of obtaining cord blood itself is not controversial, and it has saved many lives since doctors in the 1980s discovered that the umbilical cord taken from newborns is a rich source of stem cells. Although the umbilical cord is discarded after birth, a baby's parents can now allow blood to be extracted first. The blood is either stored in a private cord blood bank in case the child later needs a stem cell transplant, stored in a public cord blood bank, or donated for immediate transplant into a patient.

Although the number of stem cells in cord blood is often not sufficient to treat people larger than a small child, the cells are less likely than other types of donated ASCs to be rejected by a recipient. In 1988 doctors in Paris, France, performed the first successful cord blood transplant on a six-year-old boy with the blood disease Fanconi anemia, and since then physicians have used cord blood to cure thousands of people who had a variety of

A close-up view shows a unit of cryopreserved human cord blood. Stem cells from cord blood are less likely than adult stem cells to be rejected by a recipient.

blood diseases and cancers. As the author of *The Stem Cell Divide* points out, "Yet again, the common theme in the development of cellular therapy is the conversion of tissues thought to be 'medical waste' into medical gold mines."[39]

Although no one has questioned the ethics of using cord blood to save lives, a related technique pioneered by doctors at the University of Minnesota in 2000 has generated immense controversy. This method involves parents who have a child in need of a stem cell transplant and who conceive IVF embryos for the purpose of selecting one that can develop into a baby whose cord blood cells will be compatible for transplant into the ill child. After the embryos are conceived in a laboratory, preimplantation genetic diagnosis tells the parents which embryo will not only be free of certain genetic diseases, but also will be most genetically compatible with the sibling. The parents then choose to have that embryo implanted in the mother's womb. After the baby is born, its cord blood cells are used to treat the sibling.

SELECTING AN EMBRYO FOR A CORD BLOOD TRANSPLANT IS JUSTIFIED

"God gave us this technology. God gave us Adam and God gave Molly her second chance at life, and to us that was what was morally and ethically right."—Lisa Nash, mother of Adam Nash, who was conceived so his umbilical cord stem cells could save his sister Molly's life

Quoted in CNN Health. "Genetic Testing of Embryos Raises Ethical Issues." June 27, 2001. http://articles.cnn.com/2001-06-27/health/embryo.testing_1_genetic-diagnosis-genetic-testing-genetic-defect?_s=PM:HEALTH.

The first couple to employ this method of embryo selection was Jack and Lisa Nash, whose six-year-old daughter, Molly, had Fanconi anemia, a rare genetic disease that prevents people from creating bone marrow. Without a stem cell transplant, Molly would have died. The Nashes underwent IVF and selected an embryo that did not have the genetic defect that causes Fanconi anemia and that was a tissue match for Molly. When baby Adam was born, doctors led by oncologist John Wagner infused stem cells taken from Adam's umbilical cord into Molly, who was cured.

The case unleashed a firestorm of controversy over the ethics of selecting an embryo to benefit another child. Many bioethicists previously supported the idea of using PGD to screen for genetic diseases, but this use of PGD opened a new range of ethical concerns, even though the technique involved no pain or risk for Adam. Bioethicist Jeffrey P. Kahn of the University of Minnesota stated in a *New York Times* article, "We've crossed the line that we really never had crossed before, selecting based on characteristics that are not best for the child being born, but for somebody else. Nobody wants babies to be born strictly for the parts they would create. But by the same token I don't think we're willing as a society to ask people why they're having children and to say, 'That's not a good enough reason.'"[40]

In the same article, Lisa Nash stated that she and her husband had wanted another child anyway, and indeed had been trying IVF even before they heard about the new University of Minnesota PGD selection method. "You could say it was an added perk to have Adam be the right bone marrow type, which would not hurt him in the least and would save Molly's life. We didn't have to think twice about it,"[41] she said.

SELECTING AN EMBRYO FOR A CORD BLOOD TRANSPLANT IS WRONG

"The central problem with PGD [is that] human life is considered merely a product and of so little value that one child will be created to be 'used' by another."—Louise Harbour of Action Life

Louise Harbour. "Choosing the Perfect Child: What's Wrong with PGD." Action Life. www.actionlife.org/life-issues/fetal-research-and-reproductive-tech/pre-natal-diagnosis/267-choosing-the-qperfectq-child-what's-wrong-with-pgd.html.

In a 2010 Minnesota Medical Foundation article celebrating Molly Nash's tenth year following her cure, Wagner spoke about what he considered to be the most important concern: saving lives. "We knew this was going to be a hotly contested ethical issue," said Wagner. "But we also knew that it was Molly's best chance. . . . This technology is now being used for many different diseases, and many places offer it. While the debate continues, we use these technologies for good."[42]

Stem Cells from Placenta and Amniotic Fluid

While the use of umbilical cord blood stem cells is widely employed, using the placenta and amniotic fluid as a stem cell source is still experimental because scientists were not even aware that these places harbored stem cells until around 2007. Doctors can collect amniotic fluid, the liquid that surrounds a developing fetus, with a needle during pregnancy to check cells shed from the fetus for genetic diseases if the parents wish to have this done. The procedure is considered safe, though it does carry a slight risk of harming the fetus. In 2007 researchers led by Anthony Atala of Wake Forest University in North Carolina showed that some of the cells found in amniotic fluid are stem cells that can differentiate into all three embryonic germ layer cells. Atala named the cells amniotic fluid–derived stem (AFS) cells. AFS cells differ somewhat from other pluripotent cells in that they do not produce the same proteins and do not form teratomas. However, researchers believe AFS cells are an easily obtained, noncontroversial potential source of therapeutic stem cells. "Our hope is that these cells will provide a valuable resource for tissue repair and for engineered organs as well," Atala says in a *Guardian* article. "These cells are capable of extensive self-renewal, a defining property of stem cells. They can also be used to produce a broad range of cells that could be valuable for therapy."[43]

In 2010 scientists in Japan obtained mesenchymal cells, which are ASCs that develop into bone, muscle, fat, and connective tissue, from another part of the placenta—the amniotic membrane that lines the placenta. They injected these cells, called human amniotic membrane–derived mesenchymal stem cells (hAMCs), into rats after the rats experienced heart attacks. The cells developed into heart muscle cells and improved the rats' heart function 34 to 39 percent. The cells also survived more than four weeks before the rats' immune systems rejected them. The American Heart Association explains that this delayed rejection was probably

> because the amniotic sac is a barrier between a woman and her developing fetus. To help prevent either of their immune systems from attacking the other as foreign tissue, the amniotic membrane between them does not produce the proteins that immune systems use to identify foreign tissue. This means the usual tissue-type matching needed prior to transplantation would not be needed if hAMCs were used. Drugs to suppress the immune system also might not be needed after transplant."[44]

Plus, the Heart Association points out, the amniotic sac, along with the rest of the placenta, is routinely discarded as medical waste after childbirth, so this source of stem cells is likely to be noncontroversial.

Places Where Adult Stem Cells Hide

AFS cells and hAMCs may not only represent newly found sources of difficult-to-find ASCs; they may also indicate that ASCs are capable of developing into cell types other than the tissues from which they come. Scientists originally believed that ASCs were differentiated enough to be multipotent and to migrate only to their area of origin when injected into a recipient. For instance, they originally thought transplanted hematopoietic (blood) stem cells could only migrate to a recipient's bone marrow. But research on AFS cells and hAMCs indicates otherwise, and in addition, researcher Catherine Verfaillie and her colleagues at the Stem Cell Institute in Belgium have demonstrated that hematopoietic cells can differentiate into many types of cells, such as muscle, blood vessel, and nerve cells, when properly coaxed with chemical growth factors in a laboratory. Verfaillie coined the term multipotent adult progenitor cells (MAPCs) to describe cells that are more differentiated than ESCs, but still able to differentiate into cells of all three germ layers.

Using AFS cells, hAMCs, and MAPCs may be useful in overcoming the potency limitations of ASCs, and other research seeks to overcome the issue of limited ASC quantities by locating other areas in the body where ASCs can be found. One challenge in isolating ASCs is that they look very much like other body cells—in fact, they cannot be distinguished under a microscope. Indeed, individuals who decry the fact that some scientists have hyped the potential of immediate cures from stem cells have pointed out that these scientists have underplayed the difficulties involved in obtaining adequate supplies of ASCs.

Recently, though, scientists have made some progress in developing tests that identify chemical markers that uniquely characterize either stem cells or non-stem cells. Glycoprotein receptors are one type of markers that are present on the surface of non-stem cells. Laboratory technicians tag glycoprotein receptors by introducing a protein called a fluorescent ligand into a group of cells

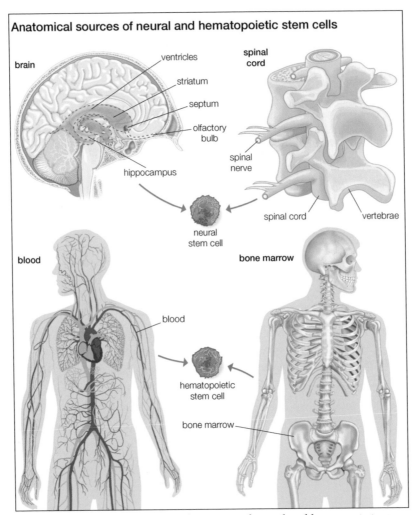

Anatomical sources of neural and hematopoietic stem cells

An anatomical illustration depicts the sources of neural and hematopoietic stem cells. Hematopoietic stem cells can differentiate into many types of cells, such as muscle, blood vessel, and nerve cells.

taken from a person's body. The fluorescent ligand binds to glycoprotein receptors and causes the cells to light up. A machine called a fluorescence-activated cell sorter then separates lit-up cells from other cells. This machine can isolate one stem cell from over one hundred thousand cells in less than an hour. Other laboratory tests being developed tag gene expression patterns, hormones, or enzymes that distinguish stem cells from other cells in an attempt to locate new sources of stem cells. Identifying multiple markers on stem cells and non-stem cells gives researchers methods of verifying not only whether or not a cell is a stem cell, but also gives clues as to the types of cell that are present (neural, blood, and so on).

Induced Pluripotent Stem Cells

As well as exploring new methods of obtaining and using adult and embryonic stem cells, scientists are also busy investigating the use of the iPSCs that were first developed in 2007. Researchers create iPSCs by reprogramming mature cells, usually skin cells, to a pluripotent state, using transcription factors such as Oct4, SOX2, KLF4, and c-Myc. These chemicals are inserted into cells with viruses, which by nature can penetrate cells. But these viruses sometimes cause cancer, so their use poses safety questions.

THE THERAPEUTIC POTENTIAL OF INDUCED PLURIPOTENT CELLS IS OVERRATED

"The regulators demand such a lot of evidence for every single cell line that's intended for therapy that it is totally impractical to have patient-specific IPS cells for treatment."—Robin Lovell-Badge of the National Institute for Medical Research in London

Quoted in Mark Henderson. "Medical Potential of IPS Stem Cells Exaggerated, Says World Authority." *Times* (London), February 17, 2010. www.timesonline.co.uk/tol/news/science/medicine/medicine/article7029447.ece.

Despite the risks, many experts believe iPSCs are promising because they can create patient-specific cell lines that would not be rejected, and many believe the value of iPSCs in drug development and basic laboratory research exceeds that of ESCs. James Thomson, for example, writes, "For transplantation therapies based on these cells, with the exception of autoimmune diseases, patient-specific iPS cell lines should largely eliminate the concern of immune rejection."[45]

In discussing the potential of iPSCs for basic research, Markus Grompe, director of the Oregon Stem Cell Center, states in a *Weekly Standard* article that:

> iPS cells are clearly superior to embryo-derived stem cells.
> . . . Direct reprogramming techniques make it possible to
> generate pluripotent cells from specific individuals with
> particular diseases. For example, it will be possible to
> make pluripotent cells from children with Fanconi's ane-
> mia, a devastating genetic disease, and study the effects of
> candidate drugs on the formation of human blood.[46]

Many people, particularly those opposed to ESC research, also believe that iPSCs have eliminated the need for ESC research and will thereby banish the related controversies. Joseph Panno is one scientist who holds this belief, and in his book *Stem Cell Research*, he discusses why he thinks many researchers are reluctant to abandon ESC research: "The reluctance of the science community to let go of human ES cell research sounds like an empire builder's lament: So much time and energy has been spent on it, so many careers have depended on it—we cannot let it go. But whether scientists want to admit it or not, iPS cells, with their infinite potential, have already made therapeutic cloning and ES cell research obsolete."[47]

THE THERAPEUTIC POTENTIAL OF IPS STEM CELLS IS IMMENSE

"Reprogramming adult tissues to embryonic-like states has count-less prospective applications to regenerative medicine, drug development, and basic research on stem cells and developmental processes."—Charles A. Goldwaite Jr. of the National Institutes of Health

Charles A. Goldwaite Jr. "The Promise of Induced Pluripotent Stem Cells (iPSCs)." National Institutes of Health. http://stemcells.nih.gov/info/2006report/2006CChapter10.htm.

Soon after the introduction of iPSCs in 2007, a variety of media reports proclaimed that the controversies about ESCs were over. In one such report, journalist Ryan T. Anderson wrote, "The stem cell wars are over. Leading scientists are telling us that they can pursue the most promising stem cell research without using

Liposuction a Potential Source of Adult Stem Cells

In 2010 researchers at Thomas Jefferson University Hospital in Philadelphia succeeded in creating blood vessels from adult stem cells found in rabbit fat cells. They obtained the fat cells using liposuction and grew the stem cells they extracted on a structural frame of human veins in a laboratory. They then transplanted grafts containing the stem cell–vein combination into the rabbits' heart arteries. Eight weeks later, the grafts remained healthy.

The investigators believe the technique has potential applications for human heart and leg artery bypass surgeries in people with clogged arteries. Doctors now use blood vessels taken from elsewhere in patients' bodies, or synthetic blood vessel grafts if no healthy blood vessels can be found. But synthetic grafts often become clogged within months or years. It appears that grafts made from stem cells remain clog-free longer.

Not only may this technique offer a solution to artificial graft complications, but it may also represent a new, easily obtained source of adult stem cells. As researcher Stephen E. McIlhenny told the American Heart Association, "Fat cells are easily obtained with liposuction. Bone-marrow-derived stem cells require going into the bone canal to take bone marrow out, which can be painful."

Quoted in American Heart Association. "Tissue Engineered Grafts Composed of Adult Stem Cells Could One Day Replace Synthetic Vascular Bypass Grafts." www.newsroom.heart.org/index.php?s=43&item=1003.

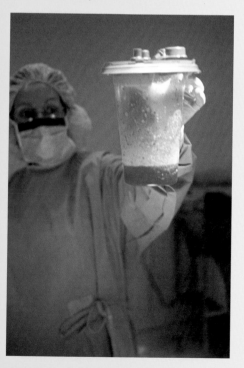

A doctor holds a receptacle containing fat removed during a liposuction procedure. Researchers believe that fat cells obtained by liposuction may be a potential source of adult stem cells.

—much less killing—human embryos."[48] But despite such proclamations, most experts have since concluded that iPSCs will not do away with the need for ESC research. IPSCs have also generated new ethical controversies of their own.

The vast majority of scientists and bioethicists now believe that research on ESCs should continue because iPSCs may not prove to be as safe or promising as expected. In an April 2011 article in *Science Progress*, bioethicist Arthur Caplan of the Center for Bioethics at the University of Pennsylvania states:

> Making adult cells into embryo-like cells remains the current darling of critics of research involving embryos. But the technique is barely understood and its safety is a huge concern to those working in the area. Not only was it hype to declare in 2007 that the game was over for embryonic stem cells or even to continue to say in 2011 that there is no need to pursue embryonic stem cell research (note, by the way, no cures from iPS—five years and counting) is nothing less than unadulterated hype driven by an agenda utterly disconnected from the nascent state of the science.[49]

Thomas Okarma, chief executive of Geron Corporation, which recently began clinical trials with human ESCs, states in a 2010 newspaper article that he believes the potential of iPSCs is limited for other reasons that make continued research with ESCs essential. "IPS cells have been talked up as therapy by people with no experience in developing therapies," says Okarma. "There is simply no business model for getting treatments based on your own cells into your body. The degree of difficulty in getting regulatory approval is just too great when you're making new therapeutic cells from scratch every time."[50] Okarma also points out that the cost of actually producing a new cell line for each patient would be unrealistically prohibitive.

Recent research has also led iPSCs into the realm of controversy. In 2009 two teams of scientists in China and one team led by Kristin Baldwin at the Scripps Research Institute in La Jolla, California, used mouse iPSCs derived from skin cells to produce embryos that developed into healthy adult mice. The studies proved that iPSCs are indeed pluripotent, and the investigators hope their discovery can be used to grow replacement organs, as well as to allow the creation of cellular models of disease.

But creating embryos without using oocytes is also a new form of cloning, which in itself is controversial. People concerned about the possibility of cloning human beings have already voiced their opposition to using iPSCs in this way. Whether the 2009 discovery will lead to restrictions on iPSC research remains to be seen, but as this type of research moves forward, new controversies emerge, and older ones are far from being resolved.

CONTROVERSIES OVER CLONING

The fact that several aspects of stem cell research involve cloning has introduced another controversial element into an already contentious field of science. Cloning refers to different processes used to duplicate biological material, such as a cell, tissues, or an entire organism. Most of the time, scientists clone isolated genes and cells to study them in a laboratory or to manufacture medicines. This is not controversial. But when scientists use the cloning technique called somatic cell nuclear transfer (SCNT) to create embryos for the purpose of extracting stem cells, it is extremely controversial. Scientists call this practice "therapeutic cloning" to differentiate it from reproductive cloning, a process that also uses the SCNT technique but for a different purpose: to duplicate an entire organism. The vast majority of individuals, as well as all the major world religions, vehemently oppose reproductive cloning, and because some of the technologies used in therapeutic cloning are similar to those in reproductive cloning, some believe both methods are highly unethical. Many also raise ethical concerns about creating and destroying embryos for no other reason than to obtain embryonic stem cells.

What Do Therapeutic and Reproductive Cloning Involve?

In SCNT, a woman donates an oocyte, and scientists remove the cell nucleus and replace it with the nucleus of a cell taken from elsewhere in her body. The new nucleus is returned to a pluripotent state and fused to the empty oocyte with a mild electric shock. This leads the newly formed cell to begin dividing and developing into a blastocyst. The inner cell mass is then removed to obtain stem cells, which are then placed in a cell culture. Scientists say SCNT has an advantage over obtaining ESCs from IVF embryos because a stem cell line obtained through SCNT is genetically identical to the donor, so it would not be rejected in a transplant. However, as with IVF-derived ESCs, SCNT kills the embryo.

While reproductive cloning also uses SCNT, its goal is to reproduce an entire organism rather than to generate ESCs. In 1902 the German embryologist Hans Spemann pioneered reproductive cloning by using a strand of hair to split apart the two cells of an early salamander embryo. Normal salamanders grew from each cell. In the late 1920s Spemann used nuclear transfer to place the nucleus of one salamander embryo cell into another embryo cell whose nucleus he had removed. The new cell developed into a normal salamander.

THE NEED TO DISTINGUISH THERAPEUTIC AND REPRODUCTIVE CLONING

"Therapeutic cloning has enormous potential. So to throw these two things out in the same motion is very unfortunate."—Biologist Rudolf Jaenisch, a professor at the Massachusetts Institute of Technology and a founder of the Whitehead Institute for Biomedical Research

Quoted in *NOVA* Online. "On Human Cloning." www.pbs.org/wgbh/nova/baby/clon_jaen .html.

Other scientists subsequently cloned other animals using nuclear transfer, but it was not until 1996 that the Scottish embryologist Ian Wilmut succeeded in cloning a mammal—a sheep named Dolly. Wilmut transferred the nucleus of an adult sheep skin cell into an oocyte whose nucleus had been removed. He then fused the skin cell nucleus and oocyte together with a jolt of electricity and implanted the resulting cell into a mother sheep, which carried Dolly to birth. Dolly and her genetic mother were thus identical twins.

Dolly: The Cloning of a Sheep, 1996

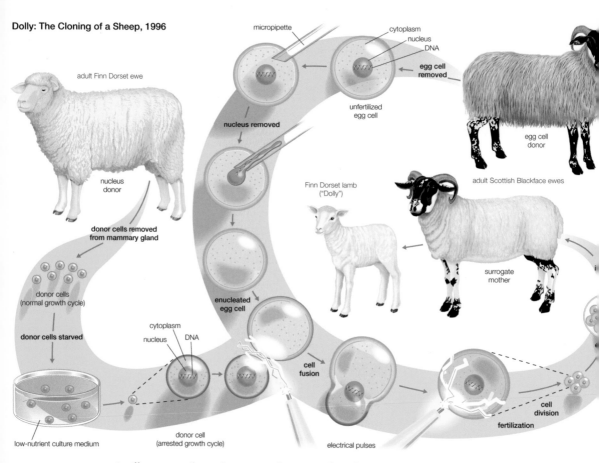

An illustration shows the process that Scottish embryologist Ian Wilmut used to clone Dolly the sheep.

The technique was inefficient—Wilmut tried it on 277 embryos and obtained one live birth—and its safety has been widely questioned because cloned animals often have severe medical problems and birth defects. Dolly herself seemed fine for several years but had to be euthanized at age six because she developed a serious lung disease.

Controversies over Reproductive Cloning

Controversies over reproductive cloning have centered on these safety issues and on the unsettling possibility of cloning human beings. According to the National Human Genome Research Institute, "Many of the concerns about cloning have focused on issues related to 'playing God,' interfering with the natural order of life, and somehow robbing a future individual of the right to a unique identity."[51] The Catholic Church, for example, states, "Human cloning is immoral because it attacks the dignity of human procreation and because it is an affront to the dignity of the individuals involved in cloning."[52]

THERAPEUTIC CLONING IS WRONG

"Before long, we'll be harvesting body parts from fully formed people. Once you begin this concept of utilitarian use of cells, then everything is up for grabs."—Religious broadcaster Pat Robertson

Quoted in BBC News. "Row over Made-to-Order Stem Cells." July 12, 2001. http://news .bbc.co.uk/2/hi/science/nature/1434894.stm.

Many opponents of reproductive cloning have argued for a worldwide ban on research that could lead to human cloning. Some countries have implemented such bans, but thus far the United States has not, despite recommendations by numerous scientists, bioethicists, religious groups, and politicians. One proponent of a ban on human reproductive cloning is Wilmut. When asked in a 2008 interview with *Scientific American* magazine whether human cloning is a potential risk, Wilmut replied:

The thing that provides the most protection at the present time is the sheer inadequacy of the technology. But I've thought about this, and I think you're right that it would become a risk at some stage. I was one of a group of people led by Bernie Siegel to try to get human reproductive cloning made a crime against humanity. I think it would be entirely appropriate to get a ban at the present time because there is a very significant risk of dead babies or of children with severe abnormalities. The list of abnormalities which we've seen in livestock and in mice is very long and quite horrifying if you think of it in terms of children.[53]

The Bernie Siegel mentioned by Wilmut is a Florida attorney who founded and directs the nonprofit Genetics Policy Institute. The group advocates for therapeutic cloning but opposes reproductive cloning, and it works tirelessly to inform the public and lawmakers about the differences. In 2003 Siegel mobilized hundreds of scientists, patient advocates, and government leaders to convince the United Nations not to implement a ban on all forms of cloning.

Attempts to Clone Humans

Despite the fact that most scientists and other people oppose human reproductive cloning, several scientists and groups of human cloning advocates exist, and the fears they generate have been responsible for much of the opposition to cloning in general. Panayiotis Zavos is one scientist who claims he knows how to clone humans safely, and in 2004 he advertised that he implanted a cloned human embryo into a woman's womb. Experts doubt the truthfulness of Zavos's claims, since no proof has emerged and since he has been known to make many misleading statements, but Zavos continues to do human cloning research at his Kentucky-based facility.

A nonscientist, Randolfe Wicker, who founded Clone Rights United Front to advocate for human cloning as a method of defying death, has also stirred up debate. According to Wicker's mission statement, "Every person's DNA is his or her personal property. To have that DNA cloned into another extended life is part and parcel of his or her right to control his or her own reproduction."[54]

But Rudolf Jaenisch, a professor of biology at the Massachusetts Institute of Technology and a renowned stem cell researcher, expresses in a *NOVA* article the consensus among scientists and ethicists that individuals like Zavos and Wicker are dangerous. Writes Jaenisch:

> There is no way to predict whether a given clone will develop into a normal or abnormal animal. Likewise, there is no way at present to predict whether a human clone will turn out to be a normal or abnormal individual. . . . Is there any good research on human cloning

being done? No. Are there any responsible scientists doing this? No. Are these cloning activists even competent
scientists? No, they're not. So with all these unknowns,
with these people at this stage proposing to do human
cloning is ludicrous. It is obvious to everyone in the scientific community that it shouldn't be done.[55]

*In 2004 scientist Panayiotis Zavos claimed to have successfully implanted a
cloned human embryo into a woman's womb; however, experts doubt the
truthfulness of this claim.*

Objections to All Forms of Cloning

Although the embryos used in therapeutic cloning cannot develop into mature organisms, many oppose this technology because they view all cloning as a form of reproduction and as morally wrong, regardless of the aim. National Right to Life spokesperson David Prentice exemplifies this viewpoint when he writes:

> If the cloned embryo is implanted in an attempt at live birth, it is termed "reproductive cloning," whereas if the same embryo is instead disaggregated for its embryonic stem cells, the process is termed "therapeutic cloning." Proponents of the latter insist it is different than the former. But both are cloning, only in one instance the embryo is implanted in a womb, in the other it is killed by extracting stem cells.[56]

Some scientists have argued that opposition to both forms of cloning has resulted from a lack of understanding of the differences. For instance, in *Stem Cell Now*, scientist Christopher Thomas Scott states, "The belief that therapeutic cloning means making humans—rather than cells—continues to be a common misunderstanding."[57]

But whether this opposition comes from equating therapeutic and reproductive cloning or from being morally opposed to both, many scientists have implored policy makers to maintain a distinction between the two and to enforce a ban on reproductive cloning, but not on therapeutic cloning. For example, after then president George W. Bush proposed a ban on both forms of cloning, stating in his 2006 State of the Union address, "Tonight I ask you to pass legislation to prohibit the most egregious abuse of medical research: human cloning in all its forms,"[58] neuroscientist Michael Gazzaniga lamented Bush's decision to reject therapeutic cloning. Gazzaniga wrote:

> Calling human cloning in all its forms an "egregious abuse" is a serious mischaracterization. This makes it sound as if the medical community is out there cloning people, which is simply not true. The phrase "in all of its forms" is code, a

The Origins of Therapeutic Cloning

The idea of therapeutic cloning developed out of new technologies for somatic cell nuclear transfer and embryonic stem cell research. According to Christopher Scott Thomas, the author of *Stem Cell Now* :

> The twin trajectories of somatic cell nuclear transfer (SCNT) and embryonic stem cell (ESC) research collided big time in 1998. . . . The intersection of the two technologies raised the stunning possibility that nuclear transfer could be used to make a custom-matched line of embryonic stem cells—in essence, a reserve of cells cloned from anyone who needed them to replace a diseased or injured part of their body.

Christopher Thomas Scott. *Stem Cell Now.* New York: Penguin, 2006, p. 50.

way of conflating [combining] very different things: reproductive cloning and biomedical cloning. . . .

[The] Bioethics Council (of which I am a member) in 2002 made a big distinction between the two forms of cloning. We voted unanimously to ban reproductive cloning. . . . We cited many reasons, from biomedical risk to religious concerns to the flat-out weirdness of the idea. . . .

At the same time, the council had differing views on biomedical cloning, including stem cell research. . . . The majority, 10 of the 17, did not call for a ban on biomedical cloning—and this was our advice to the president. Obviously, he ignored it.[59]

Bush's proposed legislation, however, did not pass in Congress.

Rather than citing their opposition to all forms of cloning, some individuals opposed to therapeutic cloning base their objections on the fact that they believe creating an embryo just to harvest its stem cells is wrong. Even some individuals who support research using discarded IVF embryos oppose creating SCNT embryos for the purpose of obtaining stem cells. For example, bioethicists George J. Annas, Arthur Caplan, and Sherman Elias write:

> Although the destruction of a human embryo is lamentable, there is a considerable moral difference between creating and destroying embryos solely to obtain stem cells and destroying unwanted human embryos that will never be used for reproductive purposes. The former involves the creation solely for the purpose of destruction whereas the latter involves salvaging something of value from a situation from which nothing else can be gained.[60]

Bioethicists Thomas Douglas and Julian Savulescu dispute this assessment and discuss in an *EMBO Reports* article why they believe creating embryos for research or therapy is not morally wrong:

> Most of us think it is permissible to produce embryos through IVF knowing that some might be destroyed for no better reason than because it is impractical to store them indefinitely. If it is permissible to produce embryos in such circumstances, then surely it is also permissible to produce embryos that might be destroyed in research. In that case, not only will the embryo be destroyed for a stronger reason—to advance medically important research, rather than to free up freezer space—but they will also be produced for what is arguably a weightier reason—to advance medically important research, rather than to meet the desires of parents for children.[61]

Fallout from a Case of Fraud

The social acceptance and legal use of therapeutic cloning has been further called into question by a case of fraudulent research that rocked the scientific world in 2005, after South Korean researcher Hwang Woo Suk announced that he had cloned the first human embryos and extracted custom-matched embryonic stem cells. Scientists hailed Hwang's achievement as a major breakthrough in the potential use of therapeutic cloning to cure disease, and Hwang became a national hero in South Korea. But in late 2005 a scandal erupted when researcher Gerald Schatten of

Gerald Schatten (right) and Hwang Woo Suk pose together at a news conference in 2005. Hwang was later convicted of embezzling, research fraud, and illegally buying human embryos after it was discovered he had faked the results of his research on cloning and stem cells.

the University of Pittsburgh, who collaborated with Hwang's team, severed his ties with Hwang after being informed of numerous ethical and scientific irregularities in the research.

Investigators revealed that some of the women who Hwang claimed had donated their eggs for the research had been forced to do so, while other women were illegally paid as much as fourteen hundred dollars for their eggs. The results of the experiments were also proved to be fabricated, and Hwang was later convicted of embezzling millions of dollars from donors and from the South Korean government, of research fraud, and of illegally buying human embryos.

Even though strict oversight, peer review, and experiment replication by other researchers provides a built-in system of checks and balances that most often prevents scientists from faking results or misusing funds, Hwang's downfall led many people to question scientists' ethics in general. The journal *Science*, which published Hwang's study, vowed to enhance their scrutiny of articles submitted for publication. Many people also believed the scandal would be especially damaging to the already controversial field of stem cell research. Eve Herold, director of public policy research and education at the Genetics Policy Institute and one of the Americans sent to Korea to help investigate the case, writes, "I was concerned that the opponents of stem cell research were being handed a reason to lob accusations of unethical behavior at every stem cell researcher in the world."[62] Indeed, many critics of therapeutic cloning, such as Richard Doerflinger of the U.S. Conference of Catholic Bishops, stated that the Hwang scandal proved therapeutic cloning was impractical, at best, and should be stopped. But stem cell and therapeutic cloning research has continued, albeit with added caution, since experts believe the potential for creating patient-specific stem cells and organs is too promising to ignore.

Controversies over Chimeras

But as this research advances, other controversies emerge. Another therapeutic cloning–related debate involves chimeras—organisms that contain more than one set of genes. In Greek mythology a chimera was a monster with the head of a lion, the body of a goat, and the tail of a serpent. In modern research, chimeras are animals that contain some human DNA or stem cells for research purposes. Scientists introduce pieces of human DNA or human stem cells into laboratory animals for several reasons. One is to create models of human diseases in these animals, so the diseases can be studied and treatments tested. Other times human cells are transplanted into animals to determine whether the cells can be used safely and effectively to treat certain diseases in a living organism. A third use of chimeras is as a source of transplantable animal organs that contain human cells and would thus be less likely to be rejected by a human patient. Animal organs, such as pig hearts and heart valves, are already used in stopgap transplants for desperately ill people until a human organ can be found.

Chimeras are also created to obtain SCNT-derived ESCs. Because human oocytes are difficult to obtain, scientists have developed methods of using SCNT to create mostly human embryos by fusing human DNA with animal oocytes. In 2006, for example, researchers at Newcastle University in England pioneered a method of removing the DNA from cow oocytes and replacing it with human DNA. They then extracted stem cells from the resulting embryos.

REPRODUCTIVE CLONING SHOULD BE MADE A CRIME

"The advantage of getting it made a crime against humanity is that there would then be no escape. No matter where you did it, it would be a crime."—Scottish scientist Ian Wilmut

Quoted in Sally Lehrman. "Is It Time to Give Up on Therapeutic Cloning? A Q&A with Ian Wilmut." *Scientific American,* July 22, 2008. www.scientificamerican.com/article .cfm?id=therapeutic-cloning-discussion-ian-wilmut.

Scientists can also create mature chimeras—fully grown animals with some human characteristics. For instance, Irving Weissman and his colleagues at Stanford University created mice with human immune systems so they could study AIDS and mice with partly human brains in order to study neurological diseases. Another researcher, Esmail Zanjani of the University of Nevada, injected human stem cells into fetal sheep and found that the sheep developed mostly human organs. Many people have expressed alarm over both the creation of SCNT chimeras and mature human-animal mixtures because they believe scientists now have the ability to create monsters, and many have argued that all such research should be halted. Stanford University professor William Hurlbut, for example, raised his concern that Zanjani's experiments would be even worse if the sheep developed visible human parts, such as human limbs or genitals, rather than internal human organs. "Human

Bernard Siegel and the Raelians

Attorney Bernard Siegel, founder and director of the nonprofit Genetics Policy Institute, advocates for ethical research using therapeutic cloning but seeks to ban human reproductive cloning because of its dangers. In 2002 Siegel made headlines when he filed a lawsuit after a company called Clonaid claimed they had cloned a human baby named Eve. The lawsuit asked a court to appoint a temporary guardian for Eve, since Siegel believed no sane parents would clone a child and that the baby needed protection. The trial revealed that neither baby Eve nor Clonaid actually existed. The entire story about Eve was a fraudulent money-generating scheme perpetrated by a group called the Raelians, whose leader, Rael, claims to be from another planet and preaches that he came to Earth to give humans immortality through cloning. The Raelians continue to claim that they are cloning babies in their laboratories, but no one has ever seen the babies or the facilities.

Attorney Bernard Siegel speaks to the media following a hearing on Baby Eve, supposedly the first cloned human baby.

appearance is something we should reserve for humans," Hurlbut says. "When we start to blend the edges of things, we're uneasy. That's why chimeric creatures are monsters in mythology in the first place."[63]

In an article in the *Wisconsin Medical Journal*, physician Norman Fost discusses another concern many people have about placing human stem cells into animals:

> In the worst case—and at this point imaginary—scenario, creative thinkers wonder whether a fully functioning human brain could develop inside, say, a goat, and if that did happen, should we think of it as a really smart goat, or as a human trapped in a goat's body: the so-called "Help, let me out of here" fear. Most scientists believe this is, and will remain, science fiction. They feel it is biologically highly implausible that human brain cells could organize themselves inside a goat's head and function in a sufficiently organized way to raise concerns.[64]

Another objection to research with chimeras centers on concerns that it defies the natural order of life and is an affront to human dignity. "I think it would be basically immoral to create a human whose status we could not determine," Doerflinger states. "We'd have an unresolvable dilemma about how to treat this animal."[65] Alfonso Gomez-Lobo, a former member of the President's Council on Bioethics, puts forth the view that chimeras violate the sanctity of human life by mixing humans with animals. He states, "What is essentially human is really debased."[66]

BOTH FORMS OF CLONING ARE WRONG

"I believe all human cloning is wrong, and both forms of cloning ought to be banned."—George W. Bush, forty-third president of the United States

Quoted in National Right to Life Committee. "In Historic Speech, President Bush Urges U.S. Senate to Ban Human Embryonic Cloning, but Democratic Leader Backs Embryo Farms," April 14, 2002. www.nrlc.org/Killing_Embryos/Bushurgescloningban.html.

Majority of Americans Support Therapeutic Cloning

Therapeutic cloning is the use of cloning technology to help in the search for possible cures and treatments for diseases and disabilities. Do you think research into therapeutic cloning should be allowed to go forward?

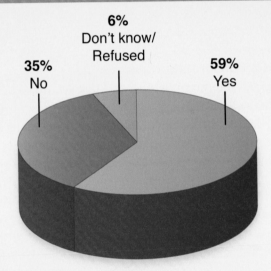

6%
Don't know/
Refused

35%
No

59%
Yes

Taken from: Taking Our Pulse, The *Parade*, Research!America health poll, June 2005. Charlton Research Company for Research!America.

Based on such moral arguments, in 2009 Senators Sam Brownback and Mary Landrieu introduced a law that would prohibit the creation of chimeras, but the law did not pass in Congress. Other countries, however, such as Canada, have instituted bans on chimeras, and some U.S. lawmakers hope to revisit the issue, along with proposals to ban any sort of cloning. Such legal and political oversight of these issues, along with the regulation of other stem cell–related research, plays a big role in the controversies and progress of this area of science.

WHO SHOULD REGULATE SCIENTIFIC AND ETHICAL DECISIONS?

Many aspects of the controversies over stem cells revolve around disputes about the role government and religion should play in regulating, or making rules for, medical research and treatments. Since health care issues affect both individuals and society, relevant decisions have historically been shared by lawmakers, doctors, scientists, theologians, and patients themselves. Few people dispute the fact that ethical regulations are necessary, but differences of opinion arise about the extent of government power and the influence of religion and public opinion on this oversight, or supervision.

The Need for Regulation

Government involvement in ethics policy and medical research stems from historical abuses of people by scientists. Horrific experiments conducted on concentration camp victims in Nazi Germany were extreme examples of the abuses that led to the creation of the Nuremberg Code following the post–World War II Nuremberg Trials. The Nuremberg Code specifies that human participation must be voluntary and that safety rules must be followed in scientific research throughout the world.

Most nations also create and enforce their own ethical regulations. After abuses of research subjects in the famous Tuskegee, Alabama, syphilis study became known in the early 1970s, for example, officials saw the need for increased government oversight in America. In the Tuskegee case, in 1932 the U.S. Public Health

A poster contains photos of some of the victims of the Tuskegee syphilis study.

Service enrolled six hundred low-income African American men in a study in which researchers secretly infected many of the men with syphilis and monitored their progress for forty years. By the time word of the deception came out, many of the men had unknowingly infected others, and many had also died of the disease.

In 1979 the U.S. Department of Health, Education, and Welfare released a document called the Belmont Report, which described ethical guidelines for medical research. It specified, among other things, that people must give informed consent about all aspects of research studies. Informed consent means that the person, or subject, must be told about and understand all of the potential risks and must agree to take part in the research. The report also stated that researchers must uphold the subject's right to dignity and to get some potential benefit from the research. Since then, other laws have also been passed to further protect research subjects and to prevent false research claims, inappropriate use of funding, and abuses of technology.

Government Dollars for Research

One way the U.S. government regulates research is by controlling funding, or money given to support something. Most medical research in America is funded by the NIH. According to an article in *NOVA scienceNOW*, "Scientists say that no field of research can flourish without access to this kind of government support."[67] Such research is extremely expensive, since the high-tech equipment needed is very costly, and few privately funded companies are willing to risk investing a lot of money in the equipment and in the salaries of highly trained scientists. Much of the research is therefore conducted at universities and government facilities that rely on public dollars.

Most of the time, doctors and scientists oversee how these funds are spent because they have the knowledge to decide which research projects sound promising. But over the past few decades, politicians, rather than medical experts, have taken greater control over how this money may be used, particularly when an area of research is controversial. This is largely because conservative religious groups have exerted pressure on politicians not to fund research that they consider to be unethical. For example, since

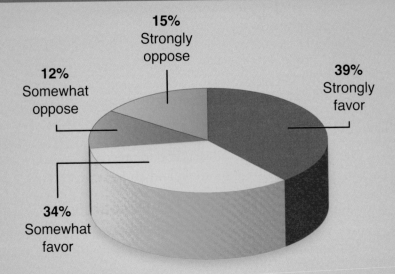

Americans Favor Expanding Federal Funding for ESC Research

Do you favor or oppose expanding federal funding for research using embryonic stem cells?

15%
Strongly oppose

12%
Somewhat oppose

39%
Strongly favor

34%
Somewhat favor

Taken from: Your Congress–Your Health Survey, June 2009, Charlton Research Company for Research!America. www.newvoiceforresearch.blogspot.com/2009_08_01_archive.html.

1995 the government has banned federal funding for any research that involves the creation or destruction of human embryos under the Dickey-Wicker Amendment, named for congressional representatives Jay Dickey and Roger Wicker. Since ESCs are not embryos, the funding ban did not apply to using stem cells during the Bill Clinton administration, as long as embryos were not created for research purposes. Then in 2001 George W. Bush signed a law that forbade federal funding for research on ESC lines derived after August 9, 2001, but allowed funding for cell lines developed from donated IVF embryos prior to this date. The Bush legislation also stated that any scientist who used any government-supplied equipment for new ESC research was subject to criminal prosecution.

Bush based this legislation on his personal conviction that while it is important to advance scientific research that could lead to cures for devastating diseases, it is also important for the government to protect human embryos from exploitation and to foster respect for life. He announced in a speech that these convictions led him to conclude that "we should allow federal funds to be used for research on existing cell lines, where the life-and-death decision has already been made."[68]

Some news accounts about the Bush ban expressed the view that Bush also signed the legislation in response to pressure from the right to life movement that supported his election. A CNN article, for example, stated, "Conservative groups had called upon Bush to stick to campaign promises to reject any federal funding for embryonic stem cell research."[69] But since the new law allowed funding for established cell lines, many news accounts debated whether this "compromise" was a victory for stem cell research advocates or opponents.

THE GOVERNMENT MUST ENFORCE A BAN ON EMBRYONIC STEM CELL RESEARCH UNDER THE LAW

"Since 1996, in what has been popularly known as its Dickey-Wicker Amendment to each HHS [Health and Human Services] Appropriations Bill, Congress has expressly banned NIH from funding research in which human embryos 'are destroyed, discarded, or knowingly subjected to risk of injury or death.'"— Advocates International, a nonprofit organization that promotes justice and religious freedom

Advocates International, September 14, 2010. www.advocatesinternational.org/blog/september14-2010-0.

When it became apparent that many of the existing cell lines were defective, however, the Bush ban put a halt to most ESC research in the United States. The lack of funding led many disillusioned scientists either to leave for other countries or to pursue other avenues of research. Some progress did occur in private companies, but in general, ESC research in America fell far behind that in other countries that had no such legal constraints, such as England, Israel, South Korea, and Singapore.

Some scientists who continued to study ESCs in privately funded research centers in the United States made an effort to share their cell lines so publicly funded scientists could continue their research, but this did not have a significant effect. Douglas Melton of the privately funded Harvard Stem Cell Institute, for instance, was so distraught by the scientific setbacks the Bush restrictions caused for most scientists that he took the bold step of starting more than seventy new ESC lines and providing them free of charge to publicly funded researchers who were not allowed to start cell lines but were not prohibited from using them.

Because the new policies significantly hampered ESC research, several states chose to fund the research on their own. In 2004, for instance, California voters approved Proposition 71, which provided $3 billion over ten years for this research. Illinois, Connecticut, Maryland, and New Jersey also began state-sponsored stem cell research programs to help advance this field.

A Reversal of the Bush Ban

On March 9, 2009, President Barack Obama issued Executive Order 13505 to reverse Bush's policy of limiting federal tax dollars for embryonic stem cell research. Obama's order cited the vast potential of the research to benefit humankind and also reiterated the government's commitment to ethical oversight, stating, "The Secretary of Health and Human Services, through the Director of NIH, may support and conduct responsible, scientifically worthy human stem cell research, including human embryonic stem cell research, to the extent permitted by law."[70]

Most scientists, along with stem cell advocates, were pleased by the new government policy. Melton, for example, praised Obama's decision and stated in *Time* magazine that he was relieved that "we can stop the silliness."[71] The "silliness" he was referring to was the need, under the Bush policy, for scientists at both publicly and privately funded institutions to document carefully the use of every single piece of laboratory equipment so they would not be prosecuted for using any government-supplied microscopes or refrigerators for anything related to ESC research.

Opponents of ESC research, on the other hand, were disheartened by Obama's new policy because they saw it as a reversal of the government's promotion of ethical research and protection

In 2009 President Barack Obama signed Executive Order 13505, which overturned former president George W. Bush's policy of limiting federal tax dollars for embryonic stem cell research.

of human embryos. National Right to Life Committee director Douglas Johnson stated, "The Obama administration today slides further down the slippery slope of exploiting non-consenting members of the human species—human embryos."[72]

In 2010 James Sherley and Theresa Deisher, backed by the conservative Alliance Defense Fund, which promotes the protection of religious freedom and the influence of Christian values on social issues, filed a lawsuit to overturn the new law and to block funding for any ESC research. A judge ordered funding halted while the lawsuit proceeded, but the government appealed this ruling, and funding continued during the appeal. In April 2011 a federal appeals court overturned the first judge's ruling and cleared the way for funding to continue indefinitely. Sherley and Deisher, in turn, plan to take the case to the Supreme Court.

A GOVERNMENT BAN ON EMBRYONIC STEM CELL RESEARCH IS WRONG

"How can these politicians allow needless suffering because they care more about cells in a dish than they do about people like me?"—Paraplegic Susan Fajt

Quoted in Eve Herold. *Stem Cell Wars.* New York: Palgrave MacMillan, 2006, p. 104.

Sherley, a biological engineer with the Boston Biomedical Research Institute, and Deisher, research director of AVM Biotechnology in Seattle, claim in their suit that federal funding for ESC research violates the Dickey-Wicker Amendment by allowing the creation and destruction of human embryos (which the Dickey-Wicker Amendment prohibits), and also depletes funds available for the research they are conducting on iPSCs. In a Reuters news article, Sherley states, "Not only is human adult stem cell research being compromised by the funding diverted to human embryonic stem cell research, so is all other ethically responsible human disease research."[73]

In November 2010 Sherley's employer opposed his lawsuit and joined the case in support of NIH funding for ESC research because the employer believes the lawsuit is harmful to scientific progress. Other organizations and researchers have also decried the legal wrangling. Clive Svendsen, director of the Regenerative Medicine Institute at Cedars-Sinai Medical Center in Los Angeles, states in a *Modern Healthcare* article, "No matter who wins in court, the effort to develop therapies out of human embryonic stem cells has been set back years because of the uncertainty regarding highly valued federal funding of the research."[74]

Politics and Research

Many scientists have expressed the viewpoint that these controversies over government control of funds for ESC research are the unfortunate result of nonscientists being given too much power to make what the scientists believe should be scientific decisions. While acknowledging that government oversight is necessary, especially as modern science stretches the boundaries on ethical issues involving life and death, these scientists are frustrated by what they view as regulations formulated for political reasons, such as rewarding certain religious groups for their support in an election. In *Stem Cell Wars*, Gerald Fischbach, dean of the faculty of medicine at Columbia University Medical Center, states that he is alarmed by the fact that government officials' funding decisions are being swayed by religious beliefs, rather than by principles that can be scientifically proved. Says Fischbach, "When you begin arguments based on convictions that are not open to scientific discourse, the whole process starts to crumble, and that worries me, not only with stem cells but with the whole sphere of scientific inquiry. . . . There are more and more regulations of science for political reasons. I think it is very threatening."[75]

Experts point out many instances in recent years, particularly under former president George W. Bush, where personal political agendas have determined science policy decisions. In 2004, for example, Bush fired several members of the President's Council on Bioethics (which is supposed to offer diverse opinions to the president on biomedical issues) who did not agree with his personal views on stem cells. After council member Elizabeth Blackburn, a prominent biologist, was fired and replaced with someone who agreed with Bush's views, Blackburn told the *Washington Post*, "I think this is Bush stacking the council with the compliant."[76] Blackburn said this because she believed that Bush was only allowing people whose views agreed with his own to stay on the council so he could then assert that the council backed his decisions.

Another example of politics trumping science occurred in 2005, after Bush vetoed a congressional bill to expand federal funding for ESC research. Bush held a news conference with several babies that had been adopted from discarded frozen IVF embryos and encouraged Americans to adopt all of the four hundred thousand frozen surplus embryos rather than allowing them to be used for research. Critics pointed out that not only was it the sole

Biologist Elizabeth Blackburn believes she was fired from the President's Council on Bioethics because she did not agree with President George W. Bush's views on embryonic stem cell research.

Government and Ethics

Former president George W. Bush's Executive Order 13435, dated June 20, 2007, spelled out restrictions on federal funding for embryonic stem cell research. The following clause exemplified Bush's belief that ethics should be legislated by the government:

> It is critical to establish moral and ethical boundaries to allow the Nation to move forward vigorously with medical research, while also maintaining the highest ethical standards and respecting human life and human dignity; the destruction of nascent life for research violates the principle that no life should be used as a mere means for achieving the medical benefit of another; human embryos and fetuses, as living members of the human species, are not raw materials to be exploited or commodities to be bought and sold; and the Federal Government has a duty to exercise responsible stewardship of taxpayer funds, both supporting important medical research and respecting ethical and moral boundaries.

Federal Register. "Executive Order 13435—Expanding Approved Stem Cell Lines in Ethically Responsible Ways." http://edocket.access.gpo.gov/2007/pdf/07-3112.pdf.

right of the genetic parents to decide the fate of the frozen embryos, but Bush had not bothered to mention that the vast majority of these genetic parents chose to donate surplus embryos for research rather than giving them to prospective adoptive parents, so the adoptions he urged were not even a possibility.

There is also evidence that many political leaders make regulatory decisions based on political posturing to satisfy campaign donors, such as the National Right to Life Committee and various religious groups that oppose embryonic stem cell research. In 2005, for example, U.S. Representative Diana DeGette stated, "There are Congressmen who, when the National Right to Life Committee calls and says 'vote this way on this bill,' they do it."[77]

Religion, Morality, and Politics

Many religious and pro-life advocates, however, argue that they have a moral duty to ensure that government policies are ethical, and that furthermore, as American citizens, they have a right to ensure that their tax dollars are spent on research they support. They consider it their duty to weigh in and exert influence on personal medical decisions such as IVF, abortion, and euthanasia and on issues such as ESC research because they believe decisions that threaten life or violate the sanctity of life as described in the Judeo-Christian Bible affect not only individuals, but society as well. A 2010 article on the Catholic online forum Opus Sanctorum Angelorum, for instance, states, "The Church, as the visible presence of Christ here on earth, has the mission to bring the truth of God's loving plan in Christ not only to individuals, but also to peoples and nations, to every aspect of human life, including the social, economic and political dimensions."[78]

But many people believe it is wrong for the views of religious groups to hold such power over political and medical decisions. Many pro–ESC research advocates also claim that most Americans support this research, and that it is wrong for the views of a minority to have such extensive influence over these decisions. This claim comes from polls such as one conducted in 2010 by *U.S. News & World Report*, which found that 72 percent of Americans support ESC research, and that 69 percent of Catholics and 58 percent of evangelical Christians are among these supporters.

RELIGIOUS LEADERS HAVE A DUTY TO INFLUENCE SOCIAL POLICY

"The Church has the right and the duty to advocate a social order in which the human dignity of all is fostered, and to protest when it is in any way threatened."—Basil Hume, former archbishop of Westminster

Quoted in Catholic Church in England and Wales. The Common Good and the Catholic Church's Social Teaching. www.catholic-ew.org/uk/content/download/2013/13442/file/THE%20COMMON%20GOOD%20AND%20THE%20CATHOLIC%20CHURCH_1996.pdf.

Opponents of ESC research, however, challenge the validity of this poll, stating that in other polls, such as an International

Communications Research poll, which inform respondents that embryos are killed to obtain ESCs, almost 70 percent of the respondents opposed government funding for such research. Another poll that gave information on alternatives to ESCs found that 47 percent of the respondents opposed public funding.

RELIGIOUS VIEWS SHOULD NOT DICTATE THE COMMON GOOD

"It does not follow that the theology of a few should be allowed to forestall the health and well-being of the many. And how can we affirm life if we abandon those whose own lives are so desperately at risk?"—Ronald Reagan Jr., son of the late, former U.S. president Ronald Reagan

Quoted in Michael Bellomo. *The Stem Cell Divide*. New York: AMACOM, 2006, p. 98.

Whether or not a majority or a minority of Americans favor ESC research, many doctors, scientists, religious leaders, patients who have pinned their hopes on stem cell research, and politicians disagree with the attempts of religious groups to impose their views on others by influencing public policy. In a *New York Times* editorial, for example, John C. Danforth, a former Republican senator from Missouri and an ordained Episcopal minister, states, "When government becomes the means of carrying out a religious program, it raises obvious questions under the First Amendment [which mandates a separation of church and state]."[79]

The author of *Stem Cell Wars* further advances this argument when she points out that people who would not be comfortable receiving medical treatment derived from ESCs should have the right to refuse such treatment, but that they should not have the right to deny these treatments to others who choose them. "One analogy to this situation would be if Jehovah's Witnesses, who call upon their members to reject blood transfusions, could decide that no one could receive a blood transfusion. Most people would say this is unfair,"[80] she writes. But anti-ESC advocates counter such arguments by saying it is their duty to speak out to prevent ethical abuses, and that if the public is educated about how ESC research destroys embryos, they will agree that funding this research is wrong. They also point out that once society approves killing one human being to save another, there might be no end to the path on which this disregard for human life progresses. If killing embryos is acceptable, they state, would it also be acceptable to take body parts from fetuses and infants to use in medical treatments?

Scientific Regulation in Other Countries

Religious and political pressures play varying roles in research and treatment regulations throughout the world, and the resulting laws and public funding policies also differ from country to country. In England, for example, ESC and therapeutic cloning research on embryos under fourteen days old is permitted and federally funded. In other European Union countries, therapeutic and reproductive cloning are forbidden, and Germany prohibits research using surplus IVF embryos as well. England, Japan, South Korea, Israel, and Singapore are all leaders in stem cell research because all allot significant government funding while still enforcing stringent ethical guidelines.

Several countries, though, lack or do not enforce stem cell research and treatment regulations, and profit-driven scams and abuses have proliferated. In a 2010 article in the *Kennedy Institute of Ethics Journal*, philosophy professor and lawyer Cynthia B. Cohen and physician and lawyer Peter J. Cohen reveal that many patients have been lured to unregulated countries such as Russia, Mexico, India, and several African nations by doctors who claim to have developed miraculous stem cell cures for a variety of medical conditions.

The choice to seek unproven remedies lies, of course, with individual patients, many of whom are willing to risk an unknown procedure when legitimate doctors tell them nothing can be done to help them. But Cohen and Cohen argue that all countries should implement and enforce regulations to protect patients from financial and scientific exploitation: "Countries in which such unproven treatments are offered owe it to those drawn within their borders for stem cell treatments and their own citizens to regulate the provision of these dubious therapies according to internationally accepted standards for proven treatments and to enforce such regulations."[81]

One country in which unproven stem cell treatments are widely advertised on the Internet is Russia. Private clinics and even beauty salons offer embryonic, adult, placental, and umbilical cord stem cell transplants for a variety of ailments, including paralysis,

Human embryonic stem cells as seen through a light microscope. Laws regarding embryonic stem cell research vary from country to country throughout the world due to several factors, including religious and political pressures.

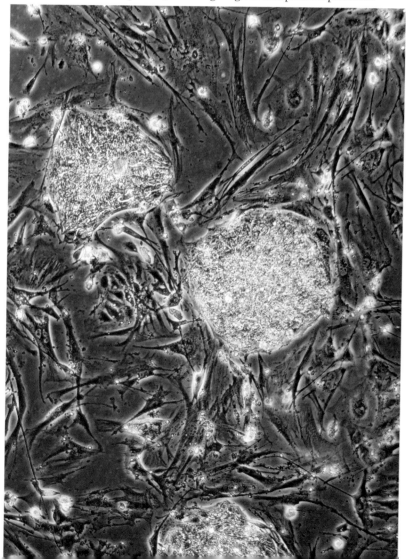

Susan Fajt Versus Representative Dave Weldon

In 2005 paraplegic Susan Fajt made headlines when she accused Florida representative Dave Weldon of illegally exploiting her for political gain. Fajt, who became a paraplegic in 2001 as a result of an automobile accident, traveled to Portugal for an experimental adult stem cell transplant procedure she hoped would enable her to walk. Doctors transplanted cells from the inside of Fajt's nose into her spinal cord, and she regained some sensation in her legs and could stand for brief stretches with the help of leg braces. Some experts believe the stem cells led to her improvement, but others have stated that cells called olfactory ensheathing glia that were transplanted along with the stem cells were probably responsible.

Despite the lack of proof that the stem cells helped Fajt, Weldon claimed in a speech to the House of Representatives that her case proved that adult stem cells could cure paralysis, and that research on embryonic stem cells was therefore unnecessary. Weldon also enlarged a photo he took of Fajt standing up and displayed it to members of Congress without her permission.

Fajt, who was in Washington to testify that she believed Congress should authorize funding for embryonic stem cell research, was infuriated that Weldon used her photo and exploited her story to generate support for his own anti–embryonic stem cell agenda. She wrote a letter demanding that he apologize and stop using the photo, and she stated in a newspaper article, "If Weldon wouldn't have used me and said a cure is going to be found with adult stem-cell research, embryonic stem-cell research may have been federally funded." Weldon stopped using the photo, but he did not apologize.

Quoted in Kristen Philipkoski. "Stem-Cell Patient Roasts Lawmaker." *Wired*, June 3, 2005. www.wired.com/med tech/health/news/2005/06/67728.

Susan Fajt (right), a paraplegic who has been treated with stem cells, listens as Dr. Irving Weissman testifies before a Senate Committee on stem cell research.

Parkinson's disease, multiple sclerosis, and facial wrinkles. No one, however, knows whether or not stem cells are actually used. Even if they are used, safety has not been established, and stories of harmful effects abound. An American doctor who received a purported ESC treatment for multiple sclerosis at a Moscow clinic worsened and became confined to a wheelchair. A man who sought stem cell treatments for gray hair and wrinkles developed tumors from the injections he received. An Israeli boy whose parents brought him to Russia for neural stem cell injections to treat a rare neurological disease developed tumors in his brain and spinal cord.

Legitimate Russian doctors and scientists, as well as doctors and scientists worldwide, have protested against these stem cell clinics and have demanded a government crackdown, since not only do such clinics endanger lives, they also fuel suspicions about the ethics of other professionals involved in stem cell research and therapy. In 2005 the Russian Ministry of Health closed several unlicensed clinics, but by 2007 more than five hundred new unlicensed clinics sprang up in Moscow alone, and the government has done nothing to shut them down since they are private companies.

Similar situations exist in other unregulated countries. A doctor named Geeta Schroff, for example, has treated over six hundred patients with stem cell injections at her clinic in Delhi, India, with no oversight. The research director at the L V Prased Eye Institute in Hyderabad, India, which illegally transplants fetal stem cells into patients with eye diseases, was quoted as saying, "Guidelines are only guidelines. Any violations cannot be punished."[82]

While bioethicists and scientists worldwide believe that such abuses must be curbed, disputes about the extent to which doctors, politicians, religious groups, and public opinion should hold the power to formulate such regulations persist. Should the opinions of any or all religious groups enter into laws governing stem cell research and treatment? How much government regulation is too much? How much is too little? There are no easy answers to these questions, and related debates will no doubt continue.

CHAPTER 6

THE FUTURE OF
STEM CELL RESEARCH

With the ongoing controversies and biological hurdles facing stem cell research still to be overcome, scientists and government leaders are focusing on addressing several areas that impose barriers to future progress. One area relates to the fact that stem cell research in the United States lags behind that in other countries that have devoted much more public funding for all types of stem cell research. While the U.S. government and scientific community believe international cooperation in research is important, they are still hoping to establish the United States as a leader in stem cell research and therapy. But lawsuits challenging Barack Obama's reinstatement of federal funding for ESC research and uncertainty over whether the next president will try to reverse this policy continue to hamper research momentum, and until such issues are settled, many experts have conceded that significant progress in the United States is unlikely to occur.

Former NIH director Elias Zerhouni expresses the delicate balance government and scientific leaders must keep in advancing research to benefit people while still adhering to laws and ethical guidelines when he states, "Unfortunately, the scientific foundation of stem cell research is sometimes lost in the societal, moral, and ethical battle between hype and hope. But our job at NIH is to push the science forward to serve our patients."[83]

According to a January 2011 news article, another stumbling block for research progress in the United States is the ongoing legal and financial competition for patents. States the article: "Scientists are busily filing for legal patents that give them exclusive intellectual property rights for each discovery they make in the hopes that one day, one will lead to a blockbuster cure and big cash for those who devised it."[84] This is not a major issue in most other countries and regions of the world. In Europe, for example, a 2008 ruling prohibited patents on human ESC lines and innovations, and rather than competing, researchers are cooperating by registering new stem cell lines in an international stem cell bank and sharing them with other scientists.

Much of the competition for patents in the United States stems from the 2001–2009 ban on federal funding for ESC research. This left most research progress to profit-driven private companies rather than NIH-funded projects. Robert Lanza, chief scientific officer at Advanced Cell Technology, reveals that the race to secure patents halted some of his own research because scientists at another biotechnology corporation managed to obtain a patent before he did. Lanza worked on using ESCs to reverse diabetes in animals for many years but was unable to continue because Geron Corporation received an exclusive license to use ESCs for diabetes. "You just have this complete minefield out there and you know who the victims are? It's the patients. Here I was, a scientist trying to cure diabetes and I couldn't use my entire lifetime of expertise to try and develop that technology,"[85] he says.

Overcoming Scientific Challenges

In addition to promoting the progress of stem cell research, scientists seek to overcome the technical and safety challenges to improve future prospects for viable therapies. Recent progress in developing methods of making stem cells proliferate in cell cultures, differentiate into desired cell types, stay alive and function normally in a recipient after transplant, and avoid rejection or tumor formation have helped shape future research directions and in some instances raised new questions about the possibilities of eventual treatments.

One significant concern about stem cell cultures centers on the use of human or mouse feeder cells as nourishment. The risk that these feeder cells contain disease-causing bacteria and viruses has led scientists to seek culturing methods that do not require feeder cells. In 2010 researchers at the Karolinska Institutet in Sweden developed a technique of growing human ESCs using a

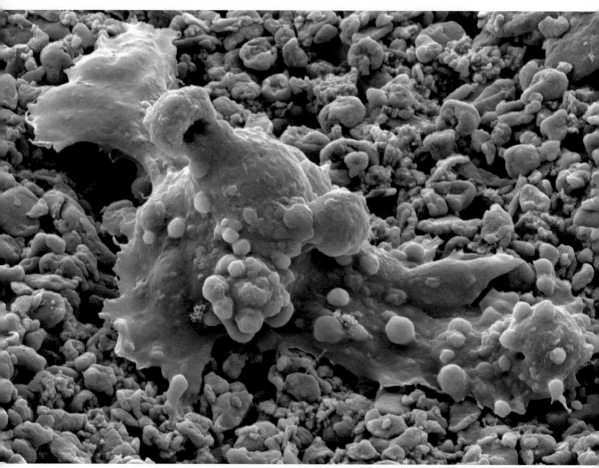

A colored scanning electron micrograph showing green embryonic stem cells on their grey feeder cells. One significant concern about stem cell research is the risk that these feeder cells contain disease-causing bacteria and viruses.

single human protein called laminin-511. Although laminin, which is found in connective tissue, is difficult to extract, the scientists pioneered a method of producing it artificially using gene cloning. They believe that using laminin in cell cultures will open the door to making ESCs safe for transplantation.

Another problem with stem cell cultures has been the fact that ASCs do not grow easily. In 2010 a team led by Colleen Delaney at the Fred Hutchinson Cancer Research Center in Washington made headway in stimulating umbilical cord stem cells to proliferate in a laboratory. The researchers used chemicals that activate a cell mechanism called the Notch signaling pathway, which regulates cell growth. They then infused the expanded stem cell populations into leukemia patients, and the cells took only about two weeks to engraft and start producing new blood cells. This was much faster than usually occurred with the limited quantities of cord blood stem cells previously available, so the technique appears to have immediate therapeutic applications if it proves to be safe.

Directed Differentiation

Another challenge is directing embryonic and iPS cell differentiation into specific types of precursor cells before they can be transplanted. If the cells are not partially differentiated before injection, they form teratomas. If they are completely differentiated, on the other hand, they will not proliferate or migrate to appropriate body tissues.

Scientists have made progress in determining which types of chemical growth factors trigger partial differentiation of certain cell types. Nerve growth factor, for example, seems to stimulate differentiation of stem cells in all three germ layers, whereas fibroblast growth factor works on ectoderm cells, and transforming growth factor works on mesoderm cells. Different combinations of growth factors also seem to be effective for triggering differentiation into specific cell types.

In 2009 researchers at the National Institute of Arthritis and Musculoskeletal and Skin Diseases discovered an entirely new method of inducing mouse ESC differentiation into muscle cells. They used a type of RNA called microRNA-214, which controls gene expression in cells, to block a protein called EZH2. EZH2 keeps stem cells undifferentiated. If this method proves to be more efficient than using chemical growth factors, it may hasten the progress of ESC therapies.

Clinical Trials

Although RNA-directed differentiation is not yet being used to prepare ESCs for use in humans, scientists are using recent progress with chemical growth factors to launch the first human

ESC clinical trials in the United States. In 2010 the U.S. Food and Drug Administration granted two private companies permission to begin studies on a small number of people. Advanced Cell Technology received approval to transplant stem cells into people with Stargardt's disease, a rare form of childhood blindness, and Geron Corporation began to test ESCs on people with spinal cord injuries.

Since 2010 a small number of patients with spinal cord injuries, such as T.J. Atchison (pictured), have been treated with embryonic stem cells in order to study the effects the stem cells have on the patients' paralysis.

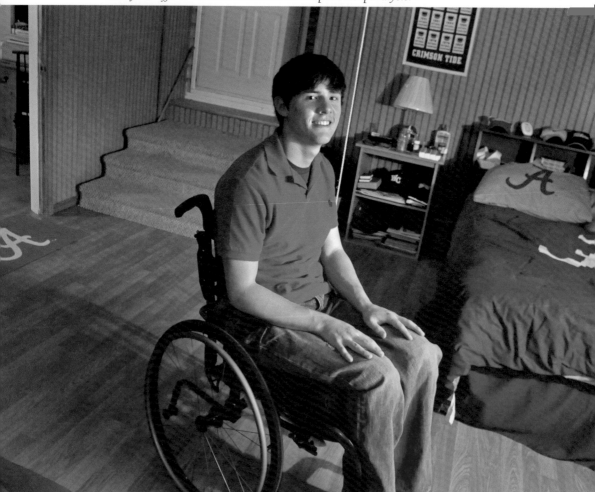

Other research is using new methods of directed differentiation of ASCs and iPSCs to assess their safety and effectiveness in treating many diseases, including AIDS, sickle-cell anemia, lupus, arthritis, diabetes, and others. Some studies are also evaluating optimal quantities of stem cells needed to ensure engraftment and to minimize the risk of rejection.

BOTH EMBRYONIC AND iPSC RESEARCH MUST CONTINUE

"The best and most current scientific and medical data establishes that research on all forms of stem cells, including human embryonic stem cell research, is vital to understanding disease mechanisms and developing new therapies for many currently untreatable diseases."—International Society for Stem Cell Research

International Society for Stem Cell Research. "ISSCR Statement On U.S. Court Decision to Overturn Ban on Federal Funding of Human Embryonic Stem Cell Research," April 29, 2011. www.isscr.org/Ban_on_hESC_Research_Funding_Lifted1/3053.htm.

In other clinical trials, physician and researcher Anthony Atala and his colleagues at Wake Forest University are using both embryonic and adult stem cells to create custom body organs and are testing their products in people. They have built functioning bladders, kidneys, blood vessels, and uteruses and are working on livers, pancreases, and other complex organs. The team grows the stem cells on protein scaffolds to give them structure, then engineers them into organs. They are also developing custom organ patches and skin for burn victims using a machine similar to a computer scanner/printer. The machine contains an inkjet cartridge loaded with skin stem cells. After scanning a burn patient's tissue, the machine prints out sheets of new skin cells to lay over the damaged tissue.

Atala emphasizes that both embryonic and adult stem cells are crucial for his research, since different kinds of stem cells work best for making different organs. "If a heart has an infarct [damage], engineering new tissue from embryonic stem cells is best, because trying to biopsy a bit of the heart in order to isolate [adult stem] cells for tissue engineering endangers the patient,"[86] he explains in *Stem Cell Now*.

Progress with Induced Pluripotent Stem Cells

Although some scientists believe progress with adult and iPSC has supplanted the need for ESC research, most experts, including Anthony Atala, think that research with all three cell types must and will continue in the future, since each offers advantages for specific laboratory research and therapeutic applications. But since iPSCs and ASCs are far less controversial than ESCs are, many scientists are forging ahead with research related to them in hopes of overcoming biomedical safety issues so noncontroversial disease treatments may quickly become available.

One concern about iPSCs comes from research reported in 2010 by Lanza. His team found that although iPSCs could be directed to differentiate into several cell types, the resulting specialized cells aged and died prematurely. This raises questions about the reliability of iPSCs in basic research and their safety in disease treatments, and future research will continue to explore the issue.

Other safety issues revolve around the gene-altering viruses used to reprogram cells back to pluripotency. These viruses can alter cell DNA and lead to cancers, so researchers are working on developing new reprogramming methods that do not require viruses. In 2010 Derrick Rossi of the Harvard Stem Cell Institute pioneered a way of using RNA molecules for this purpose. He used synthetic messenger-RNA to instruct skin cells to reprogram into pluripotent cells and called the cells RNA-iPS (RiPS) cells. Since messenger-RNA does not enter cellular DNA the way viruses do, there is little chance of it leading to DNA mutations or out-of-control cell replication. Using messenger-RNA is also more efficient than using viruses. Reprogramming with viruses leads to a 0.0001 to 0.01 percent success rates, whereas Rossi's technique resulted in a 1 to 4 percent success rate.

In a *Harvard Science* article, Harvard Stem Cell Institute codirector Douglas Melton says, "This work by Derrick Rossi and his colleagues solves one of the major challenges we face in trying to

A group of iPSCs in a laboratory refrigerator cools down after incubation.
Scientists have cautioned that iPSCs should not yet be tested on humans since
research has indicated that the body's immune system can perceive the cells as
foreign tissue and attack the cells.

use a patient's own cells to treat their disease. I predict that this
technology will immediately become the preferred method to
make iPS cells from patients."[87] Rossi plans to take the next step
in his research—inducing RiPS cells to differentiate into specific
cell types—in the future.

Although some experts have stated that Rossi's innovation is a
strong indication that the safety issues involving iPSCs can be overcome, NIH director Francis S. Collins cautions that this does not di-
minish the need for ESC research to continue, nor does it address

The Future of Stem Cells

In his book *Stem Cell Now*, bioethicist Christopher Thomas Scott points out that the full potential of using stem cells to cure disease will not be realized for many years. Says Scott:

> Unfortunately, the reality of stem cell biology is overshadowed by the hype. For example, the future is imagined to hold an inexhaustible source of stem cells with a perfect genetic match banked at a local hospital, available for your every medical whim. Need a new pancreas? Place your order and, three weeks later, a new one lies ready and waiting in the surgical suite. Heart failure? No worries—a few injections with multipotent stem cells will grow new cardiac tissue. Thus, many twenty-first century patients are imagined to extend their lives—through a kind of patchwork medicine, held together by a fabulous, potent cell. This future sounds incredibly exciting. But it will take time—and vision—to get us there. . . . Developing a new therapy goes slowly and is terribly expensive—discovering, testing, and manufacturing one new drug can take between 10 and 15 years and cost nearly a billion dollars.

Christopher Thomas Scott. *Stem Cell Now*. New York: Penguin, 2006, pp. 96–97.

other iPSC safety concerns. "This research in no way reduces the importance of comparing the resulting iPS cells to human embryonic stem cells," Collins states. "Previous research has shown that iPS cells retain some memory of their tissue of origin, which may have important implications for their use in therapeutics. To explore these important potential differences, iPS research must continue to be conducted side by side with human embryonic cell research."[88]

Other recent findings support Collins's claim that research on all types of stem cells should continue, since thus far, none seems to be risk free. In May 2011 researchers led by Yang Xu at the University of California–San Diego reported that implanting iPSCs into mice triggered severe immune reactions. Although this may prove not to be true in humans, Xu stated that before doctors experiment with placing iPSCs into people, scientists must carefully reconsider the prevailing viewpoint that iPSCs will not provoke an immune response. Xu believes that, somehow, in turning a mouse's mature cells into pluripotent stem cells, something changes in the cells that can lead the immune system to perceive the cells as foreign tissue.

EMBRYONIC STEM CELL RESEARCH IS UNNECESSARY

"If noncontroversial stem cells are available, why not use them instead of ES [embryonic stem] cells?"—Biologist Joseph Panno

Joseph Panno. *Stem Cell Research*. New York: Checkmark, 2010, p. 161.

Other recent research may lead to methods of getting around such problems. Several scientists have shown that mature adult cells can be turned into other types of cells without first making them pluripotent. In 2010, for instance, a team of Canadian researchers at McMaster University switched on the Oct4 gene to turn human skin cells into blood cells without reverting them to pluripotency. The investigators believe their innovation may have clinical applications much sooner than research using iPSCs does, since switching on a gene does not seem to make cells abnormal or to pose risks to patients. They reported that not only might this innovation lead to methods of custom generating blood for patients who need blood transfusions, but may also provide an accessible source of cells for people who need bone marrow transplants. Rather than relying on blood or bone marrow donations from others, doctors could take skin cells from patients and turn them into blood cells.

In similar research, in 2008 scientists at the Harvard Stem Cell Institute used a combination of transcription factors to turn pancreatic exocrine cells into insulin-producing beta cells, which functioned normally when transplanted into mice. As with the Canadian research, this may bring cell reprogramming closer to clinical applications.

Alphabet Soup

In 2010 researcher Derrick Rossi coined the latest acronym to describe the newest stem cell subtype: RiPS cells (RNA-induced pluripotent stem cells). The ever-growing list of stem cell types and subtypes includes:

Adult Stem Cells (ASCs)
• Cord stem cells (CSCs) or umbilical cord stem cells (UCSCs)
• Hematopoietic stem cells (HSCs)
• Mesenchymal stem cells (MSCs)
• Multipotent adult progenitor cells (MAPCs)
• Neural stem cells (NSCs)
• Human amniotic membrane–derived mesenchymal cells (hAMCs)

Embryonic Stem Cells (ESCs)
• Human embryonic stem cells (hESCs)
• Embryonic germ cells (EGCs)
• Human parthenogenetic stem cells (hPSCs)
• Amniotic fluid–derived stem cells (AFSCs)

Induced Pluripotent Stem Cells (iPSCs)
• RNA-iPS cells (RiPS cells)

Researcher Derrick Rossi has coined the term to describe the latest subtype of stem cell, RNA-induced pluripotent stem cells (RiPS cells).

Ongoing Scientific and Ethical Challenges

The scientific challenges that must be overcome before stem cells of all types can reach their full therapeutic potential will not be resolved overnight. Immediate and long-term safety issues take years to assess, and laboratory research and clinical trials proceed slowly out of an abundance of caution. In fact, according to the

NIH, "Stem cell research is one of the most fascinating fields of contemporary biology, but, as with many expanding fields of inquiry, research on stem cells raises scientific questions as rapidly as it generates new discoveries."[89]

So, too, will the ethical controversies related to stem cells and therapeutic cloning extend into the future. Even less controversial innovations, such as iPSCs and umbilical cord blood stem cells, ignite impassioned debates when scientists invent new uses for these technologies, such as using iPSCs to create embryos from skin cells and using preimplantation genetic diagnosis to select embryos whose cord blood can cure an ill sibling. As the frontiers of science continue to expand into issues involving the creation and maintenance of life, existing and new controversies will no doubt flourish. The author of *Stem Cell Wars* aptly expresses the outlook for the future when she states, "Without a doubt, the ethical issues raised by these fields will generate job security for bioethicists for decades to come."[90]

Introduction: Epic Discoveries and Controversies

1. Quoted in Thomas H. Maugh II. "Dr. Ernest McCulloch Dies at 84; He and Research Partner Were First to Isolate and Identify a Stem Cell." *Los Angeles Times*, February 5, 2011. http://articles.latimes.com/2011/feb/05/local/la-me-ernest-mcculloch-20110205.
2. Quoted in Gina Kolata. "Man Who Helped Start Stem Cell War May End It." *New York Times*, November 22, 2007. www.nytimes.com/2007/11/22/science/22stem.html.

Chapter 1: The Potential of Stem Cells

3. Christopher Thomas Scott. *Stem Cell Now*. New York: Penguin, 2006, p. 16.
4. NIH, "Stem Cell Basics," http://stemcells.nih.gov/info/basics/basics2.asp.
5. Michael Bellomo. *The Stem Cell Divide*. New York: AMACOM, 2006, p. 43.
6. Quoted in NIH, *Regenerative Medicine,* http://stemcells.nih.gov/info/2006report/2006Chapter6.htm.
7. Quoted in NIH, *Regenerative Medicine*, http://stemcells.nih.gov/info/2006report/2006Chapter7.htm.
8. Quoted in NIH, *Regenerative Medicine*, http://stemcells.nih.gov/info/2006report/2006Chapter3.htm.
9. Quoted in James P. Kelly. "Michael J. Fox Offers Hype over Hope." *Human Events*, October 31, 2006. www.humanevents.com/article.php?id=17770.
10. Quoted in Rebecca Morelle. "Stem Cells: Hope or Hype?" BBC News, November 9, 2006. http://bbc.co.uk/2/hi/health/6127772.stm.
11. Quoted in Steve Connor. "Gene Research Brings Schizophrenia Hope." *Independent* (UK), April 14, 2011. www.independent

.co.uk/news/science/gene-research-brings-schizophrenia- hope-2267295.html.

12. NIH, "Stem Cell Basics," http://stemcells.nih.gov/info/basics/basics6.asp.

13. Joseph Panno. *Stem Cell Research*. New York: Checkmark, 2010, p. 124.

Chapter 2: The Controversy over Embryonic Stem Cells

14. Genesis 2:7, English Standard Version.

15. Quoted in Eve Herold. *Stem Cell Wars*. New York: Palgrave MacMillan, 2006, pp. xvi–xvii.

16. Alan Malnak. "Another Look at Stem Cell Research." Michael J. Fox Foundation for Parkinson's Research, June 7, 2009. www.michaeljfox.org/newsEvents_parkinsonsInTheNews_article.cfm?ID=505.

17. Robert P. George and Patrick Lee. "Embryonic Human Persons." *EMBO Reports*, April 2009. www.nature.com/embor/journal/v10/n4/full/embor200942.html.

18. Josh Brahm. "8 Bad Arguments for Human Embryonic Stem Cell Research." Right to Life of Central California. www.rtlcc.org/fresno-madera/resources/8_bad_arguments_for_embryonic_stem_cell_research.html.

19. Quoted in Michael Specter with Gina Kolata. "After Decades of Missteps, How Cloning Succeeded." *New York Times*, March 3, 1997. www.nytimes.com/1997/03/03/us/after-decades-of-missteps-how-cloning-succeeded.html?ref=ian wilmut&pagewanted=1.

20. Jeff McMahan. "Killing Embryos for Stem Cell Research." *Metaphilosophy*, April 2007, p. 181.

21. George and Lee. "Embryonic Human Persons."

22. Scott Klusendorf. "Harvesting the Unborn: The Ethics of Embryo Stem Cell Research." Stand to Reason. www.str.org/site/DocServer/harvest.pdf?docID=150.

23. McMahan. "Killing Embryos for Stem Cell Research," p. 186.

24. George and Lee. "Embryonic Human Persons."

25. Quoted in Carl Zimmer. "Scientist at Work: Michael Gazzaniga; A Career Spent Learning How the Mind Emerges from

the Brain." *New York Times*, May 10, 2005. http://query.nytimes.com/gst/fullpage.html?res=950CE2DB1230F933A25756COA9639C8B63&pagewanted=2.

26. McMahan. "Killing Embryos for Stem Cell Research," p. 185.

27. Bertha Manninen. "Revisiting the Argument from Fetal Potential." *Philosophy, Ethics, and Humanities in Medicine*, May 17, 2007. www.peh-med.com/content/2/1/7.

28. Canadian Physicians for Life. "Cloning and Stem Cell Research," April 2001. www.physiciansforlife.ca/html/life/stemcell/articles/statementonstemcells.html.

29. Quoted in Herold. *Stem Cell Wars*, p. 39.

30. Laurie Zoloth. "What Does It Mean to Be Human?" NPR, November 22, 2005. www.npr.org/templates/story/story.php?stpryid=4867060.

31. George J. Annas, Arthur Caplan, and Sherman Elias. "Stem Cell Politics, Ethics, and Medical Progress." *Nature Medicine*, December 1999, p. 1340.

32. American Catholic. "Stem Cell Research and Human Cloning." www.americancatholic.org/Newsletters/CU/ac0107.asp.

33. Scott Klusendorf. "Embryo Stem-Cell Research Help." Stand to Reason, www.str.org/site/News2?page=NewsArticle&id=5227.

Chapter 3: Alternatives to Embryonic Stem Cells

34. Panno. *Stem Cell Research*, p. 41.

35. Quoted in Barrett Duke. "Has Robert Lanza Solved the Embryonic Stem Cell Research Dilemma?" Ethics & Religious Liberty Commission, August 25, 2006. http://erlc.com/article/has-robert-lanza-solved-the-embryonic-stem-cell-research- dilemma.

36. Quoted in Rob Waters. "Advanced Cell Makes Stem Cells Without Harming Embryo." Bloomberg, January 10, 2008. www.bloomberg.com/apps/news?pid=newsarchive&sid=agmAMjbyyX44&refer=home.

37. Quoted in Waters. "Advanced Cell Makes Stem Cells Without Harming Embryo."

38. *Zenit*. "Stem Cells and Parthenogenesis," March 2, 2011. www.zenit.org/rssenglish-31897.

39. Bellomo. *The Stem Cell Divide*, p. 168.

40. Quoted in Denise Grady. "Son Conceived to Provide Blood

Cells for Daughter." *New York Times*, October 4, 2000. www
.nytimes.com/2000/10/04/us/son-conceived-to-provide-
blood-cells-for-daughter.html.

41. Quoted in Grady. "Son Conceived to Provide Blood Cells for
Daughter."

42. Quoted in Sara E. Martin. "A Revolutionary Decision." Minnesota Medical Foundation, November 16, 2010. www.mmf
.umn.edu/bulletin/2010/fall/lookback/index.cfm.

43. Quoted in Alok Jha. "Mother's Wombs Could Provide Source
of Stem Cells." *Guardian* (Manchester, UK), January 8, 2007. www
.guardian.co.uk/science/2007/jan/08/medicalresearch.stemcells.

44. American Heart Association. "New Source of Stem Cells
Form Heart Muscle Cells, Repair Damage." May 28, 2010.
http://newsroom.heart.org/pr/aha/1047.aspx.

45. Quoted in Ryan T. Anderson. "The End of the Stem-Cell Wars."
Weekly Standard, December 3, 2007. www.weeklystandard
.com/Content/Public/Articles/000/000/014/387asfnv.asp.

46. Quoted in Anderson. "The End of the Stem-Cell Wars."

47. Panno. *Stem Cell Research*, p. 87.

48. Anderson. "The End of the Stem-Cell Wars."

49. Arthur Caplan. "The Stem Cell Hype Machine." *Science
Progress*, April 18, 2011. www.scienceprogress.org/2011/04/
the-stem-cell-hype-machine.

50. Quoted in Mike Henderson. "Medical Potential of IPS Stem
Cells Exaggerated, Says World Authority." *Times* (London),
February 17, 2010. www.timesonline.co.uk/tol/news/science/
medicine/article7029447.ece.

Chapter 4: Controversies over Cloning

51. National Human Genome Research Institute. "Cloning Embryonic Stem Cells." www.genome.gov/10004765.

52. Catholics United for the Faith. "Cloning: An Affront to Human Dignity." www.cuf.org/faithfacts/details_view.asp?ffID=195.

53. Quoted in Sally Lehrman. "Is It Time to Give Up on Therapeutic Cloning? A Q&A with Ian Wilmut." *Scientific American*, July 22, 2008. www.scientificamerican.com/article.cfm?
id=therapeutic-cloning-discussion-ian-wilmut.

54. Clone Rights United Front. "Mission Statement." www.clone
rights.com/mission_statement.htm.

55. Quoted in *NOVA* Online. "On Human Cloning." www.pbs
    .org/wgbh/nova/baby/clon_jaen.html.
56. David Prentice. "Former Cloner Now Says Cloning of No
    Practical Relevance." *National Right to Life News*, March 2,
    2011, www.nrlc.org/News_and_Views/March11/nv030211
    part2.html.
57. Scott. *Stem Cell Now*, p. 51.
58. Quoted in *Washington Post*. "President Bush's State of the
    Union Address." January 31, 2006. www.washingtonpost
    .com/wp-dyn/content/article/2006/01/31/AR2006013
    101468.html.
59. Michael Gazzaniga. "All Clones Are Not the Same." *New York
    Times*, February 16, 2006. www.nytimes.com/2006/02/16/
    opinion/16gazzaniga.html.
60. George J. Annas, Arthur Caplan, and Sherman Elias. "Stem
    Cell Politics, Ethics, and Medical Progress," p. 1340.
61. Thomas Douglas and Julian Savulescu. "Destroying Un-
    wanted Embryos in Research." *EMBO Reports*, October 2009.
    www.nature.com/embor/journal/v10/n4/full/embor20
    0954.html.
62. Herold. *Stem Cell Wars*, p. 183.
63. Quoted in Jamie Shreeve. "The Other Stem Cell Debate." *New
    York Times*, April 10, 2005. www.geneticsandsociety.org/
    article.php?id=1621.
64. Norman Fost. "The Great Stem Cell Debate: Where Are We
    Now? Cloning, Chimeras, and Cash." *Wisconsin Medical Jour-
    nal*, 2006, p. 17.
65. Quoted in Carolyn Y. Johnson. "Blending of Species Raises
    Ethical Issues." *New York Times*, April 21, 2005. www.ny
    times.com/2005/04/20/health/20iht-snchim.html.
66. Quoted in Johnson. "Blending of Species Raises Ethical Is-
    sues."

Chapter 5: Who Should Regulate Scientific and Ethical Decisions?

67. Kyla Dunn. "The Politics of Stem Cells." *NOVA scienceNOW*.
    www.pbs.org/wgbh/nova/body/stem-cells-politics.html.
68. Quoted in *Online NewsHour*. "President Bush." PBS, August 9,

2001. www.pbs.org/newshour/bb/health/july-dec01/bush speech_8-9.html.

69. CNN. "Bush to Allow Limited Stem Cell Funding." August 9, 2001. http://articles.cnn.com/2001-08-09/politics/stem .cell.bush_1_cell-funding-cell-research-cell-lines?_s=PM :ALLPOLITICS.

70. Federal Register. "Executive Order 13505—Removing Barriers to Responsible Scientific Research Involving Human Stem Cells." http://edocket.access.gpo.gov/2009/pdf/E9-5441.pdf.

71. Quoted in Alice Park. "The Quest Resumes." *Time*, January 29, 2009. www.time.com/time/health/article/0,8599,1874717, 00.html.

72. Quoted in National Right to Life. "National Right to Life Says the Obama Administration Is Pushing Step-by-Step the Creation and Harvesting of Human Embryos for Research," April 17, 2009. www.nrlc.org/press_releases_new/Release 041709.html.

73. Quoted in Maggie Fox. "Stem Cell Opponent Has Challenged Authority Before." Reuters, August 24, 2010. www.reuters .com/article/2010/08/24/stemcells-usa-sherley-idUSN2427 127520100824.

74. Quoted in Paul Barr. "Stop-and-Go Scenario." *Modern Healthcare,* March 21, 20111. www.modernhealthcare.com/article/ 20110321/ MAGAZINE/110319975&template=printpicart.

75. Quoted in Herold. *Stem Cell Wars*, p. 77.

76. Quoted in Rick Weiss. "Bush Ejects Two from Bioethics Council." *Washington Post*, February 28, 2004. www.washington post.com/ac2/wp-dyn?pagename=article&contentId=A1 3606-2004Feb27.

77. Quoted in Herold. *Stem Cell Wars*, pp. 69–70.

78. Opus Sanctorum Angelorum. "The Voice of the Church in Today's World," Summer 2010. www.opusangelorum.org/En glish/2010_2/2010_summer.htm.

79. John C. Danforth. "In the Name of Politics." *New York Times*, March 30, 2005. www.nytimes.com/2005/03/30/opinion/ 30danforth.html.

80. Herold. *Stem Cell Wars*, p. 130.

81. Cynthia B. Cohen and Peter J. Cohen. "International Stem

Cell Tourism and the Need for Effective Regulation." *Kennedy Institute of Ethics Journal*, 2010, p. 29.

82. Quoted in Cohen and Cohen. "International Stem Cell Tourism and the Need for Effective Regulation," p. 35.

Chapter 6: The Future of Stem Cell Research

83. Quoted in *MedlinePlus*. "Stem Cell Research: Unlocking the Mystery of Disease," Summer 2007. www.nlm.nih.gov/med lineplus/magazine/issues/summer07/articles/summer07pg2-3 .html.

84. Kerry Sheridan. "Rush for Patents Is Choking U.S. Stem Cell Research." Agence France-Presse, January 24, 2011. http:// news.yahoo.com/s/afp/20110125/hl_afp/healthscience usstemcellresearch;ylt=AryP.

85. Quoted in Sheridan. "Rush for Patents Is Choking U.S. Stem Cell Research."

86. Quoted in Scott. *Stem Cell Now*, p. 114.

87. Quoted in B.D. Colen. "Breakthrough in Cell Reprogram-ming." *Harvard Gazette*, September 30, 2010. http://news .harvard.edu/gazette/story/2010/09/breakthrough-in-cell-reprogramming.

88. Quoted in Colen. "Breakthrough in Cell Reprogramming."

89. NIH, "Stem Cell Basics," http://stemcells.nih.gov/info/basics/ basics1.asp.

90. Herold. *Stem Cell Wars*, p. 22.

Chapter 1: The Potential of Stem Cells

1. Why does the field of regenerative medicine hold so much hope and promise?
2. Why do pluripotent stem cells seem to offer more therapeutic opportunities than other types of stem cells do?
3. Besides being used to treat and cure diseases, in what other areas can stem cells be useful?
4. In what ways might the potential of stem cell research have been hyped or exaggerated?

Chapter 2: The Controversy over Embryonic Stem Cells

1. How are embryonic stem cells obtained for research?
2. What are some of the arguments that support the idea that embryos are human beings?
3. What are some of the arguments that support the idea that embryos are just cells?
4. Is alleviating the suffering of sick people a higher moral priority than preserving embryos? Why or why not?

Chapter 3: Alternatives to Embryonic Stem Cells

1. Why has the single-cell extraction procedure designed to create embryonic stem cell lines without destroying embryos failed to overcome ethical controversies?
2. What are some of the alternatives to using embryonic stem cells?
3. Why does the Catholic Church oppose parthenogenesis?
4. What are the arguments for and against using preimplantation genetic diagnosis to select an embryo to cure a disease in another child?

Chapter 4: Controversies over Cloning

1. How do reproductive and therapeutic cloning differ? How are they similar?
2. Besides equating reproductive and therapeutic cloning, what other objections do people offer to therapeutic cloning?
3. What impact does a scandal such as the 2005 South Korean research fraud incident have on stem cell research?
4. Is the creation of chimeras an abuse of science? Why or why not?

Chapter 5: Who Should Regulate Scientific and Ethical Decisions?

1. What ethical rules did the Nuremberg Code and the Belmont Report describe?
2. Why do some people feel obligated to ensure that the government regulates science in accordance with their values?
3. Why did scientist Douglas Melton find the Bush administration's embryonic stem cell regulations to be "silly"?
4. Why do legitimate scientists decry abuses of patients traveling to countries that lack regulations for medical research and treatment?

Chapter 6: The Future of Stem Cell Research

1. What are some of the obstacles that the United States must overcome in order to be a global leader in the field of regenerative medicine?
2. How did the 2001–2009 ban on federal funding for embryonic stem cell research contribute to the competition for patents on stem cell technology?
3. Why are methods of controlling stem cell differentiation important for future therapies?
4. Why do most scientists believe that research on both embryonic and adult stem cells is critical for developing disease treatments?

ORGANIZATIONS TO CONTACT

Action Bioscience
American Institute of Biological Sciences
1900 Campus Commons Dr., Ste. 200
Reston, VA 20191
Phone: (703) 674-2500
Fax: (703) 674-2509
E-mail: info@actionbioscience.org.
Website: www.actionbioscience.org

Action Bioscience is an award-winning educational resource that promotes bioscience literacy. It is owned and operated by the nonprofit scientific association the American Institute of Biological Sciences.

American Association for the Advancement of Science (AAAS)
1200 New York Ave. NW
Washington, DC 20005
Phone: (202) 326-6400
Website: www.aaas.org

The AAAS is a nonprofit organization that promotes scientific advances and public education about many issues, including stem cells.

American Life League (ALL)
PO Box 1350
Stafford, VA 22555
Phone: (540) 659-4171
Fax: (540) 659-2586
Website: www.all.org

ALL is an educational pro-life organization that opposes abortion, artificial contraception, reproductive technologies, and fetal experimentation. It asserts that it is immoral to perform experiments on living human embryos and fetuses, whether inside or outside of the mother's womb.

Center for Bioethics & Human Dignity
Trinity International University
2065 Half Day Rd.
Deerfield, IL 60015
Phone: (847) 317-8180
Fax: (847) 317-8101
E-mail: info@cbhd.org
Website: http://cbhd.org

The Center for Bioethics & Human Dignity is a nonprofit group established in response to a lack of Christian input in the area of bioethics. The center promotes the potential contribution of biblical values in bioethical issues, such as stem cell research. The organization produces a wide range of live, recorded, and written resources examining bioethical issues.

Coalition for the Advancement of Medical Research (CAMR)
750 Seventeenth St. NW, Ste. 1100
Washington, DC 20006
Phone: (202) 725-0339
Website: www.camradvocacy.org

The CAMR is a coalition of patient organizations, universities, foundations, and scientific societies that strives to educate the public and to advocate for the advancement of stem cell research.

Family Research Council (FRC)
801 G St. NW
Washington, DC 20001
Phone: (800) 225-4008
Website: www.frc.org

The FRC is a conservative Christian nonprofit think tank and lobbying organization formed in 1981 by James Dobson. Its function is to promote what it considers to be traditional family values and socially conservative views on many issues, including divorce, ho-mosexuality, abortion, and stem cell research. The mission of the FRC is to inform and shape the public debate and to influence public policy to ensure that the human person is respected in law, science, and society.

Focus on the Family
8605 Explorer Dr.
Colorado Springs, CO 80920
Phone: (719) 531-5181
Fax: (719) 531-3424
E-mail: help@focusonthefamily.com
Website: www.focusonthefamily.com

Focus on the Family's primary aim is to spread its views on Christianity through a practical outreach to individual families. It is active in promoting socially conservative public policy and opposes any activity it deems a threat to the traditional idea of family, including embryonic stem cell research.

Hinxton Group
1809 Ashland Ave.
Baltimore, MD 21205
Phone: (410) 614-5391
E-mail: alanr@jhu.edu
Website: www.hinxtongroup.org

The Hinxton group is an international group made up of individuals who help shape ethical policies on stem cell research. The group's website provides information on worldwide policies and stem cell research news.

International Society for Stem Cell Research (ISSCR)
ISSCR Headquarters
111 Deer Lake Rd., Ste. 100
Deerfield, IL 60015
Phone: (847) 509-1944
Website: www.isscr.org

The ISSCR is a nonprofit organization dedicated to promoting research and education on stem cells. The society provides general information on treatments, research, and ethical issues.

National Catholic Bioethics Center (NCBC)
6399 Drexel Rd.
Philadelphia, PA 19151
Phone: (215) 877-2660
Fax: (215) 877-2688
E-mail: info@ncbcenter.org
Website: www.ncbcenter.org

The NCBC strives to promote human dignity in health care and the life sciences in accordance with the teachings of the Catholic Church.

National Institutes of Health (NIH)
9000 Rockville Pike
Bethesda, MD 20892
Phone: (301) 496-4000
Website: www.nih.gov

The NIH is the primary U.S. government medical research agency and also provides information on all aspects of stem cells.

National Right to Life Committee (NRLC)
512 Tenth St. NW
Washington, DC 20004
Phone: (202) 626-8800
E-mail: nrlc@nrlc.org
Website: www.nrlc.org

Founded in Detroit in 1973 in response to the U.S. Supreme Court decision legalizing abortion, the NRLC is the largest pro-life organization in the United States. The group has local chapters in all fifty states and works to effect pro-life policies by lobbying the government.

University of Pennsylvania Center for Bioethics
3401 Market St., Ste. 320
Philadelphia, PA 19104-3308
Phone: (215) 898-7136
Fax: (215) 573-3036
E-mail: bioeweb@mail.med.upenn.edu
Website: www.bioethics.upenn.edu

The Center for Bioethics is a leader in bioethics research and a world-renowned educational and research facility.

FOR MORE INFORMATION

Books

Lauri S. Friedman. *Stem Cell Research*. Detroit: Greenhaven, 2009. Provides a guide for teens on writing critical essays on stem cell controversies.

Margaret Haerrens. *Embryonic and Adult Stem Cells*. Detroit: Greenhaven, 2009. Written for teens; discusses the issues and controversies surrounding embryonic and adult stem cell research.

Phill Jones. *Stem Cell Research and Other Cell-Related Controversies*. New York: Chelsea House, 2011. Written for teens; explores the controversies surrounding stem cell research.

Hal Marcovitz. *Stem Cell Research*. San Diego: ReferencePoint, 2010. Written for teens; explores current stem cell research and related controversies.

Internet Sources

B.D. Colen. "Breakthrough in Cell Reprogramming." *Harvard Gazette*, September 30, 2010. http://news.harvard.edu/gazette/story/2010/09/breakthrough-in-cell-reprogramming.

Betsy Querna. "Ethics, Science, and the Brain." *U.S. News & World Report*, August 3, 2005. http://health.usnews.com/usnews/health/articles/050803/3book.htm.

Science Daily. "Scientists Turn Skin Cells Directly into Blood Cells, Bypassing Middle Pluripotent Step," November 8, 2010. www.sciencedaily.com/releases/2010/11/101107202144.htm.

Websites

Everyday Mysteries, Library of Congress (www.loc.gov/rr/scitech/ mysteries/stemcells.html). The Library of Congress has a fun and informative website about stem cells.

Stem Cell Basics, National Institutes of Health (http://stemcells .nih.gov/info/basics). This government website presents easily understood information on all aspects of stem cells.

Stem Cell Transplants, TeensHealth (http://kidshealth.org /teen/cancercenter/treatment/stem_cells.html). This teen website discusses stem cells and how they are used in transplants.

Stem Cells, University of Utah (http://learn.genetics.utah.edu/ content/tech/stemcells). This university website has articles and interactive activities about stem cells and the controversies surrounding them.

INDEX

A

Abortion, 32–33, 41
  embryonic germ cells
    derived from, 50
  spontaneous, 39
Adult stem cells (ASCs), 8
  embryonic stem cells *vs.*,
    14, 14–15
  fat cells as source of, 59
  harvesting of, 16–17
  isolating, 55–57
  reprogramming of, 11
  from umbilical cord blood,
    50–52
  use of magnetic beads to
    find, 49
  See also Induced
    pluripotent stem cells
AFS (amniotic fluid–derived
  stem) cells, 53–55
Alliance Defense Fund, 84
Alzheimer's disease,
  23–24
American Heart Association,
  54–55
Amniotic fluid–derived stem
  (AFS) cells, 53–55
ASCs. *See* Adult stem cells
Aristotle, 31
Atchison, T.J., *98*
Augustine (saint), 33

B

Belmont Report (U.S.
  Department of Health,
  Education, and Welfare), 79
Blackburn, Elizabeth, 86, *86*
Blastocysts, 15, 35, 40
  IVF, establishment of stem
    cell lines from, 44–45
Bone marrow, 7
  as source of adult stem cells,
    16
Brownback, Sam, 76
Bush, George W., 83, 85–87,
  86
  bans federal funding of ESC
    line research, 80–81
  on human cloning, 75

C

Canadian Physicians for Life,
  40
Caplan, Arthur
  on creation of stem cells
    from SCNT embryos, 70
  on hype over embryonic
    stem cells, 20, 28
  on iPSCs as substitute for
    embryonic stem cells, 60
  on morality of using
    discarded embryos for
    research, 36, 42

Cardiomyocytes, *19*
Catholic Church
  on embryonic stem cell
    research, 42–43
  on extraction of cells from
    dead embryos, 47
  on human cloning, 65
  on parthenogenesis, 48–49
  view on beginning of life, 33
Chimeras, 72–73, 75–76
Christopher and Dana Reeve
  Foundation, 23
Clonaid, 74
Clone Rights United Fund, 66
Cloning
  objections to all forms of,
    68–70
  See also Reproductive
    cloning; Therapeutic
    cloning
Conception, definition of,
  33–34
Cord blood. *See* Umbilical
  cord blood

D
Deoxyribonucleic acid (DNA),
  13, 73
Department of Health,
  Education, and Welfare,
  U.S., 79
Diabetes, type 1, 19–21
Dickey, James, 80
Dickey-Wicker Amendment
  (1995), 80, 84
Disease modeling, 26
DNA (deoxyribonucleic acid),
  13, 73

Dolly (cloned sheep), *10, 11,*
  63–64
  cloning process producing,
    64
Drug testing, 26

E
EG (embryonic germ) cells,
  49–50
Embryonic germ (EG) cells,
  49–50
Embryonic stem cell lines, 9
  challenges in growing,
    95–97
  creation of, 30–31
  from dead embryos, 46–47
  establishment from single
    cells, 44–46
  from parthenogenesis, 47–49
  patenting of, 95
  patient-specific, 57
Embryonic stem cell research
  barriers to advancements in,
    94–95
  debate over morality of, 40,
    42–43
  federal funding of, 79–87,
    80
  politics and, 85–87
  public support for, 88, 89
  regulations in other
    countries on, 90–91, 93
  support for federal funding
    of, *80*
  use of iPSCs does not negate
    need for, 60–61
Embryonic stem cells (ESCs),
  91

adult stem cells vs., *14,*
  14–15
clinical trials of, 97–100
directed differentiation of, 97
ESCs derived from, use of
  chimeras in, 73
on feeder cells, *96*
first culturing of, 8–9
iPSC as replacement for, 58,
  60
in research on human
  development, 26–27
sources of, 30–31
in treatment of neural
  diseases/injuries, 23
See also Embryonic stem cell
lines
Embryos, human
  at 16-cell stage, *38*
  debate on personhood of,
    33–34, 39
  development of, 15
  establishment of stem cell
    lines without killing, 44–45
  frozen, argument over taking
    stem cells from vs.
    discarding, 42–43
ESCs. *See* Embryonic stem
  cells
Ethics/morality
  in creation of chimeras,
    76–77
  in embryo selection to
    benefit other child, 52–53
  of embryonic stem cell
    research, 40, 42–43
  embryos-as-people argument
    and, 33–34, 40

role of government in
  legislating, 87
of taking stem cells from
  surplus embryos vs.
  discarding embryos, 32, 36

F
Fajt, Susan, 92, *92*
Fanconi anemia, 50, 52, 58
Fat cells, as source of adult
  stem cells, 59
Feeder cells, 30, 95, 96
Fertilization, definition of,
  34–35
Fetuses, 32
Fibroblast growth factor, 97
Fox, Michael J., 23

G
Gene therapy, 26
Genetics Policy Institute, 66
George, Robert P., 32, 35, 37
Geron Corporation, 60, 95,
  98
Glycoprotein receptors, 55–56

H
hAMCs (human amniotic
  membrane–derived
  mesenchymal stem cells),
  54–55
Heart disease, 18–19
Hematopoietic stem cells, 16
  sources of, *56*
Howarth, Stephen, 27
hpSCs (human
  parthenogenetic stem cells),
  47–49

Human amniotic membrane–
derived mesenchymal stem
cells (hAMCs), 54–55
Human life, beginning of, 9,
32–33
Human parthenogenetic stem
cells (hpSCs), 47–49
Hwang Woo Suk, 70–72, *71*

I
In vitro fertilization (IVF), 9,
46–47
with embryo selection, to
generate cord blood,
52–53
ESCs derived from unused
embryos in, 30–31
position of Catholic Church
on, 48
Induced pluripotent stem
cells (iPSCs), 11, *101*
advantages of, 18
does not negate need for
ESC research, 60–61
progress with, 100–103
therapeutic potential of,
57–58
in treatment of neural
diseases/injuries, 23
iPSCs. *See* Induced
pluripotent stem cells
IVF. *See* In vitro fertilization

J
Jaenisch, Rudolf, 11, 63,
66–67
Janus, Jeffrey, 47, *48*

L
Laminin, 44, 95–96
Landrieu, Mary, 76
Lanza, Robert, 44, *45*, 46, 95,
100
Leukemia, 17

M
MAPCs (multipotent adult
progenitor cells), 55
McCullouch, Ernest, 8
McMahan, Jeff, 36, 37, 40
Melton, Douglas, 20, 82,
100–101
Mesenchymal cells, 54
Michael J. Fox Foundation,
23
Morality. *See* Ethics/morality
Multipotent adult progenitor
cells (MAPCs), 55

N
National Human Genome
Research Institute, 65
National Institutes of Health
(NIH), 14, 17, 79, 105
on neural stem cells in brain,
21–22
on potential applications of
stem cells, 28
National Right to Life
Committee, 68, 76, 84, 87
Neural stem cells, 22
sources of, *56*
NIH. *See* National Institutes
of Health
Notch signaling pathway, 97

O
Obama, Barack, 82, *83*, 94
Oligodendrocytes, 24
Opinion polls. *See* Surveys

P
Panno, Joseph, 29, 45, 58, 103
Parkinson's disease, 22
Parthenogenesis,
   establishment of stem cell
   lines from, 47–49
PGD (preimplantation genetic
   diagnosis), 46, 52–53
Pius IX (pope), 33
Placenta, stem cells from, 53–55
Pluripotency, 15
Polls. *See* Surveys
Potency, of stem cells, 15
Preimplantation genetic
   diagnosis (PGD), 46, 52–53
President's Council on
   Bioethics, 85–86
Pro-choice *vs.* pro-life
   positions, 41

R
Radiation, 6–7
Raelians, 74
Reeve, Christopher, 23
Regenerative (cell-based)
   medicine, 6
Religious groups
   political pressure exerted by,
      79–80, 87–88, 93
   views on personhood of
      embryo among, 33
Reproductive cloning, 10–11,
   63

controversies over, 64–66
fraudulent research on, 70,
   72–73
human, attempts at, 66–67
Research. *See* Embryonic stem
   cell research
Revazova, Elena, 47, 48
Ribonucleic acid (RNA), 13,
   97, 100–101
RNA-induced pluripotent stem
   (RiPS) cells, 100–101, 104
Roe v. Wade (1973), 41
Rossi, Derrick, 100, 101, 104,
   104
Russia, unproven stem cell
   treatments in, 91, 93

S
Savulescu, Julian, *35,* 35–36,
   39, 70
SCNT (somatic cell nuclear
   transfer), 62–63, 69
Scott, Christopher Thomas,
   21, 68, 69, 102
Shatten, Gerald, 70, *71,* 72
Siegel, Bernard, 65, 66, 74,
   74
Somatic cell nuclear transfer
   (SCNT), 62–63, 69
   See also Reproductive
      cloning; Therapeutic
      cloning
Somatic stem cells, 14
Spemann, Hans, 63
Stargardt's disease, 98
Stem cell transplantation,
   15–18, 50–51
   in diabetes, 19–21, 98–99

in heart disease, 18–19
of iPSCs, 57
in nervous system
   diseases/injuries, 21–26
in Russia, 91, 93
Stem cells
   controversies over potential
      of, 28–29
   discovery of, 8
   hype *vs.* reality of potential
      for, 25, 28, 60, 102
   qualities of, 14–15
   types of, 104
   See also specific types
Surveys
   on embryonic stem cell
      research, 88, 89
   on federal funding of
      embryonic stem cell
      research, *80*
   on therapeutic cloning, 76

T
Teratomas, 15–16, 97
Therapeutic cloning, 62–63
   for obtaining ESCs, 10
   origins of, 69
   support for, *76*
Thompson, James, 8–9, 11
Till, James, 8
Totipotency, 15

Transcription factors, 30, 57
Tuskegee syphilis study, 77, 79
   victims of, *78*

U
Ugelstad, John, 49
Umbilical cord blood, 16,
   51–52, 105
   cryopreserved, *51*

V
Virchow, Rudolf, 6, 7

W
Weissman, Irving, 73, *92*
Weldon, Dave, 92
Wicker, Randolf, 66
Wicker, Roger, 80
Wilmut, Ian, *10*, 11, 35, 63,
   64
   on criminalization of
      reproductive cloning, 73
   on risks of reproductive
      cloning, 65

Y
Yamanaka, Shinya, 11

Z
Zavos, Panayiotis, 66, *67*
Zygotes (fertilized eggs), 15

PICTURE CREDITS

ABOUT THE AUTHOR

Melissa Abramovitz has been a freelance writer for twenty-five years. She holds a degree in psychology from the University of California–San Diego and frequently writes on medical topics. Her published works include hundreds of nonfiction magazine articles for children, teens, and adults and numerous short stories, poems, educational series books, and picture books for children and teens. She is also the author of an adult novella and a book about how to write for children and teens.